KV-116-621

WHAT'S WHERE

YOUR GUIDES

SHIMEI THE SMELLI

Alright! I'm Shimei. How are ya? I'd just like to say, 'Nice one for buying this book!' I'll be guiding you through the ins and outs, the ups and downs, the highs and lows, the tops and bottoms... not that there are many bottoms in here. You get the idea. Anyway, I'll be showing you around the book, and to help me with this enormous task is Benji.

BENJI THE BOOKWORM

Hi! I'm Benji – I've managed to worm my way (geddit?) into this book because Shimei is hopeless with numbers. He also smells awful, but that's another story. When you see me holding up a sign, if you like you can get your Bible out and read the 'official' version of the story.

INTRODUCTION

The newly-appointed king of Israel was not a happy man. King Saul had only been in the job for two minutes and he was already moaning about his subjects. If a king said 'Jump!' the rest of the people were meant to ask 'How high (your highness)?' That was Saul's motto and, as the first king of Israel, he was going to make sure that the nation's different tribes understood it. He had been made their king by the prophet Samuel[1] and king he was going to be.

1 SAMUEL 13:1–15

To prove his point he sent the twelve tribes of Israel a present. Now most of us would be pleased with a telegram from the queen should we get to be 100 but the people of Asher, Benjamin, Zebulun and the rest were a bit surprised to find the postman coming up their drives with a sackful of bits of oxen.

The message was clear - well, probably not to you so let me explain. Saul was simply saying, 'Join me in the fight against our enemies or the next group of oxen to get a slice of the action will be yours!' He meant well. He wanted Israel to be top nation. The trouble was he wanted to do it *his* way not *God's*. Add to that his mood swings (from seriously depressed to very, very down) and it didn't take a genius to work out that there was trouble on the way. Samuel the prophet, who had first told Saul he could be king, could see what was brewing... and it wasn't a pot of tea.

It was the kings that caused the problem. All the other countries had kings so the

---

[1] See page 121 of *A Tent Peg, a Jawbone and a Sheepskin Rug*.

5

Israelites wanted a king. With a king you could have royal processions, festivals and parties: a bit of colour and sparkle in a drab life. The trouble was if kings were cheered too much they began to believe they were really the most important people in the world... they could do no wrong and, quite frankly, they could get along without God having a say every five minutes. But they were wrong - so, so wrong.

Now a few months down the line Samuel had to go and see Saul. He had given explicit instructions that Saul was to wait for him at Gilgal. The deal was that when Samuel got there he would do the sacrifices necessary to pray for success in whatever battle Saul had got himself caught up in.[2] It took Samuel a while to get there but he could smell trouble a mile off. Actually what he could smell was the smoke from a bonfire and - if his nostrils weren't mistaken - the aroma of newly roasted lamb.

Samuel quickened his pace. It was quite clear in the job description. *He* was the one who did the sacrifices and prayers for all occasions. *Saul's* job was to do the slaying and whatever pillaging was up

---

[2] Saul had recently killed the leader of the Philistine army. Strangely this did not go down well with the Philistines...honestly some people are so touchy.

for grabs. This is just the kind of mess you get into when you start allowing people to become king.

Samuel marched up to Saul and told him straight: 'You're off your royal rocker if you think God is going to let you get away with this one! All those dreams of handing on the crown to your nearest and dearest - forget them. When you shuffle off your mortal coil and go to that great throne room in the sky there will be another king but it won't be Jonathan the First[3] (son of Saul).'

God had someone else in mind and he knew just where to find him...

---

[3] Ie: Saul's eldest - nice lad but it was time he got himself down to the job centre and looked at the vacancy board.

ALL IN A DAY'S WORK

1 SAMUEL 16:1-13

Out in the fields nothing was stirring. The sheep lazed in the sun. There was no wind to ruffle the grass. The lion hidden just behind a rock was waiting for his moment. He crouched low and slowly raised his head. Just a little way in front, and slightly to his left, was a fine looking young lamb which was making the lion think about mint sauce. The goat he had snaffled for breakfast was rapidly becoming a distant memory, and the thought of fresh lamb sliding down his throat was enough to make him lick his lips ever so slightly, with just the hint of a smacking sound...

Hang on a minute - the smacking sound seemed louder than usual, and it was coming from behind the lion's head. More to the point, it wasn't the lion that was making it. The last thing he saw before death swept in to carry him off was his lunch galloping away over the fields. He hadn't seen the young lad approaching from behind, and the stone that had now lodged in what used to pass for his brain was certainly a complete surprise.

The young shepherd was about to start the business of skinning, filleting and keeping the good bits for himself when he heard someone calling his name.

'David, David...'
He looked up, and there was his big brother, Abinadab, rushing towards him.

'David, come quickly, Dad's got a... oh nice lion! Friend of yours?'

David began to tell the story of grappling with the lion - in his version he thought the struggle might have been a bit more touch and go - but Abinadab never gave him the chance.

'Come on,' he said. 'Samuel's here, and he wants all eight of us to be with Dad while he makes his sacrifice.'

Leaving the lion, with that stunned expression fixed permanently on his face, behind the rock, David followed his older brother back home - home to Bethlehem, the place he had lived all his life. Not the most important village in Israel (well, not yet anyway, but once the king business was settled God's way, it was going to be right up there in the lists of 'Places I have heard of', along with London, Paris, New York and Milton Keynes... but I'm getting ahead of myself).

Samuel was waiting. He had come to the house of Jesse on God's say-so. Mind you, given the job he had to do, he would rather have been facing a whole herd of lions. He knew that God had decided to find a new king to replace Saul, but he hadn't counted on being used as the messenger for this particular task. Not that he had any problems about a new king... it was how the old king might react that worried him. Saul was not well-known for his patience, tranquility and understanding. The news that Saul was about to be downsized, re-graded and offered the opportunity to pursue new career opportunities (ie sacked) was unlikely to be greeted with uncontained joy around the royal courts. Certainly not while Saul was there to hear it at any rate. Still, Samuel had promised to do what God commanded. God had said he wanted one of Jesse's sons to be the next king. So now here he was on Jesse's farm, with news for someone that life was going to be just a little bit different in the future. The problem was... which son?

It had taken a while. Jesse had paraded his seven oldest sons in front of Samuel. They were fine specimens of Israelite manhood: tall, dark and... well, some might have said handsome but none of them were really my type. As each one came under his scrutiny, Samuel knew for certain that the new king wasn't there. God had given quite clear directions, though: Jesse's Farm, Little Town of Bethlehem

10

and here he was. Samuel was prepared to wait until the right person turned up. What else was he meant to do? Any one of these seven lads could have taken part in an election for king. No doubt many people would have looked at them and thought 'Just the job' or 'Fine kingly types' or even 'Lovely muscles!' but God wasn't like many people. He wasn't looking for biceps, rugged features and a certificate in enemy-slaying. God was looking more for a 'Whatever you say, you're the boss, just say the word' kind of person. What's more, he had promised Samuel that he would let him know when he'd found the right bloke.

Suddenly Samuel heard a voice. Not a loud, speaking-from-the-heavens type of voice. More an inside-your-head, nobody-else-will-ever-believe-me type of voice. And the voice was saying 'Here he is.'

Samuel looked up and saw Abinadab coming across the farmyard. This couldn't be right - he'd already said no to him. But behind him came another boy, one he hadn't seen before. Years younger than all the rest, he was hardly out of his teens, and Samuel couldn't see him lasting two minutes in a fight with Saul. Despite all this, the voice inside his head was now saying 'Here we go.'

David looked across at the visitor. He had heard of Samuel, but never thought he would meet him. He looked every inch the priest, with his fine robes and a bottle of what David assumed was holy liquid in his hand ('Am I worth it?' he wondered). Actually, it was olive oil and it didn't stay in the bottle for long. While David was still trying to decide how you talked to God's spokesman if he came calling, the oil was tipped over his head. Samuel could well have suffered the same fate as the lion, had David's shock not been turned into amazement. As the oil began to run down David's body, seep into his clothes and lodge in all his nooks and crannies, the anger he was beginning to feel disappeared. In its place came something else - good feelings, warmth, confidence. Years later, David would tell his friends, 'It was as though God himself came to take over my life. And he came with a clear message - "Now you belong to me".'

The rest of the family watched in astonishment. Samuel was already out of the farm and on his way home before those left standing there realised what had just happened. That was what you did when you wanted to declare that there was to be a new king. That king had turned out to be the baby brother standing in front of them, with noble kingly thoughts running through his head. And just behind the noble thoughts were more important matters such as, 'Does olive oil leave a stain?'

2 THE BOY DONE GOOD

1 SAMUEL 16:14–23

It had been quite a day for David, but he was a sensible lad and the promise that one day, some time, who knows when, he would be king, didn't get the sheep fed and watered. He was content to get on with his life and let God worry about the details of coronation services and all that stuff when he was ready for it. Meanwhile, over at the royal court, King Saul was not a happy man. He couldn't sleep. He would wake up in the night terrified by the thought that something was going to get him, and he was scared to go back to sleep again in case something did. Of course if the king didn't sleep, the court officials didn't sleep. If they didn't sleep, the slaves didn't sleep. All in all, there wasn't a lot of sleeping going on. One of the officials - concerned only for the king, and with no thought of his own need for a regular eight

14

hours - suggested that what Saul needed was someone to sing him to sleep. Strangely enough, he also had someone in mind. Someone good looking, brave and God-fearing. This someone was called David. And, dear reader, you are probably rushing ahead of me thinking 'Surely not the very same David we last saw dripping with oil and avoiding naked flames in case he did that trick where a cat turns into a dog[4]?'

The very one... ain't life peculiar?

So it was that David - the King-Elect - arrived at the royal court with his harp slung across his shoulders and his music tucked under his arm. He was a great hit. Of course, most musicians don't usually rate their success by how many people they can send to sleep, but then this wasn't a normal gig. Saul liked him so much he wanted to put him on the staff as regular 'Musician in Residence'. David's songs were of the countryside, the hills and rivers, the wonder of creation and the marvellous truth that God who made it all cared deeply about the people he had created. Songs like this one:

---

[4] Well he'd go 'Woof!' - wouldn't he?

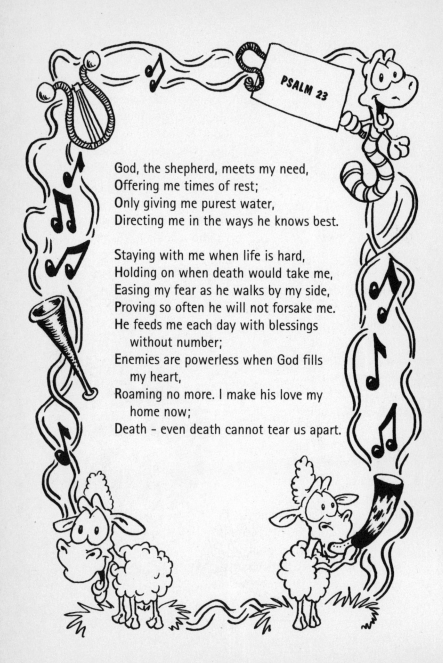

PSALM 23

God, the shepherd, meets my need,
Offering me times of rest;
Only giving me purest water,
Directing me in the ways he knows best.

Staying with me when life is hard,
Holding on when death would take me,
Easing my fear as he walks by my side,
Proving so often he will not forsake me.
He feeds me each day with blessings
    without number;
Enemies are powerless when God fills
    my heart,
Roaming no more. I make his love my
    home now;
Death - even death cannot tear us apart.

3 PEBBLE-DASHED

Life in the royal court wasn't all sleepless nights and lullabies. There were enemies to sort out (when I say 'sort out' I mean permanently - knife-to-the-throat, sword-in-the-back, end-of-story, type of 'sort out'). In particular, the Philistines were a bit of a

nuisance. When the nuisance factor got irritating, King Saul would put on his 'sorting-out' gear,

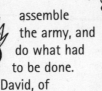

assemble the army, and do what had to be done. David, of course, was still too young to join in, so when King Saul set off to do battle, David would trot back home to do the simple things in life (tend sheep, fight off lions, kill bears... just usual everyday farming stuff). But David's brothers were in the thick of it, and it wasn't going well.

17

Every morning, Saul's soldiers were dragged out of their tents by a cry that echoed across the valleys. Not everybody has a three-metre tall Philistine soldier, dressed in bronze armour, to give them their early morning call[5]. This (big) human alarm clock had a name - Goliath. You could hear them all over the Israelite camp when they saw him for the first time, shouting 'Goli...' (pronounced 'Golly!') or words to that effect.

Goliath's morning greeting was always the same: 'Come out and fight, you...' - you can fill in the rest of the words yourself, just in case your mum is looking over your shoulder as you read this. The Israelite soldiers got the message. It was a challenge - just one of their soldiers to fight him, rather than everyone charging into battle. Surprisingly (but then again, maybe not), nobody was very keen to volunteer. Being target-practice for this giant of a man, with no chance of a re-match,[6] was not what they'd imagined when they signed up for the army. Their minds had been filled with glorious marches to victory, late nights singing triumphant songs having crushed the enemy, and fast-track promotion to a better class of tent. Their career plans didn't include rolling out of bed to be flattened by this genetically-modified muscular fighting machine.

That's what David's brothers told their youngest family member when he turned up with fresh food and news from

---

[5] Not everyone would want one: where would you put him? How much would replacement batteries cost? Did he come with a three year warranty... ? These things matter.
[6] But to be fair you'd get a top-grade funeral with full military honours.

19

home. David was disgusted. 'Are you telling me that in the whole of this army, which God has promised to be with, there isn't one of you willing to stand up to this... this... quite large person with a quite large sword?' Even King Saul's best offer couldn't do the trick - whoever defeated Goliath was promised a royal marriage, and the chance to enjoy that great privilege of royalty throughout the ages: no taxes[7]. The stampede to take up the challenge was noticeable only by its absence.

David let his scorn be heard right round the camp. Words such as 'lily-livered layabouts', 'scaredy-cat squeamish squealers' and 'air-headed army anoraks'[8] could be heard coming from his lips throughout the day. The soldiers weren't too happy about this half-time hippy harpist coming along telling them how to do their jobs. After all, they'd never suggested he play his songs in another key, or tried to change the words of his greatest hits[9]. One of David's brothers tried to get him to shut

---

[7] That's taxes – as in money to pay – not taxis, which weren't going to be invented for several thousand years.

[8] David wasn't sure what an anorak was as they hadn't been invented either, but it began with an 'A' so he let it go.

[9] It is rumoured that one of the soldiers suggested that he play 'Over the hills and far away' but this might simply be idle gossip.

up, but he wouldn't. There was an idea forming in David's mind. He had dealt with bears and lions – surely this Philistine was just another animal (with not quite as much hair). The more he thought about it, the more convinced he became that he was the man for the job.

Saul was not happy when David suggested that he would be ideal to go out and handle the 'negotiations' with Goliath. The king was obviously concerned about placing such a young innocent on to the path of certain death, and not at all bothered about losing his favourite singer – I'm sure the prospect of more sleepless nights, with only the taunts of Goliath to look forward to, had no bearing on his response at all.

GULP!

David was firm. 'I won't take no for an answer, and I'll go whether you want me to or not.' Not quite the way to talk to a king in polite society, but what could Saul do? There was nobody else rushing to sort out the problem, and so eventually Saul agreed, adding, 'You'd better take my armour.' It was a kind offer, but David and Saul weren't exactly twin brothers, separated at birth, in the body mass department. Saul was huge and David was... well, a bit smaller really. David's head rattled inside the helmet, Saul's sword was too heavy for him to lift and as for the armour – the colour didn't match his eyes. 'Thanks, but no thanks,' said David, and went out of the camp carrying a little bag, a sling[10], a stick and a few pebbles. Those who saw him go were already composing the obituary for the Israeli Daily Star. If they'd already bought David his birthday present, they would have been off down the shops waving their receipt and asking for a refund.

Goliath could not believe his eyes when he saw this young lad coming out to face him. He stared at the stick he was carrying and roared with laughter. 'This is it? This is the best you people can do?' David smiled to himself, and with only the slightest hint of nervousness, told this overgrown hairy giant with bad breath, 'I'm not afraid, and I'm not alone. God is with me, and I'm quite prepared to do my best.[11]' David got into his stride. 'If there's going to be any knocking down, any heads knocked off or any feeding to the birds - I'll be the one that's doing it.' He continued in this way for some minutes, while reaching inside his bag for the pebbles he had picked up earlier.

SUCH A LOVELY LAD!

YEAH! DEAD NICE!

---

[10] Ed. – Old-fashioned catapult.
[11] You see David knew something very important in life – however good (or not so good) your best is, with God on your side, you will always do better than your best.

Had Goliath ever come across the phrase, 'Sticks and stones may break my bones', he would no doubt have been humming it to himself right now. Mind you, he would have regretted it. Not that he had time to do much humming or regretting. The stone flew out of David's sling and smacked Goliath right between the eyes. Following the, as yet, undiscovered principle that no two objects can occupy the same space at once,[12] the stone sank inside Goliath's head as what passed for his brain dribbled out through his nose. He was dead before he hit the ground. Just to make sure, David ran over and chopped his head off with Goliath's own sword. I could make a really cheesy joke about Goliath losing his head in the heat of battle, but I won't bother...

---

[12] Ed. – Ask a science teacher.

The Philistines were stunned -
but not too stunned to run away as
fast as they could before this young
giant-killer remembered that he'd still
got four more pebbles in his bag. The
Israelites set off in hot pursuit, returning
only when they were convinced that the
Philistines were well out of the way.
They helped themselves to all
the rich pickings that the
Philistines had left behind.
All David kept was
Goliath's
weapons and
Goliath's head.
The weapons?
Fair enough. But
the head? Yeuucccch!

Not that anybody was about to argue with him - they'd seen what he could do when he put his mind to it.

'Who was that masked stranger?' Saul might have asked, had he been born several thousand years later. Instead, he simply watched the young boy wandering away from the battleground bouncing Goliath's head as he went, and demanded to know his name. Imagine his surprise when he discovered that his young harp player was a multi-tasking, stone-slinging giant-killer. Saul had him welcomed into the royal household, and David soon struck up a friendship with Saul's son and heir Jonathan. Whether Jonathan ever talked of his dreams of being king one day, and whether David let him in on the secret, history does not tell us. Nevertheless, remember that friendship, for the time was coming (and coming soon) when David would be pleased that he had at least one person he could rely on in the royal family.

4 FATHER OF THE BRIDE

1 SAMUEL 18

The Philistines had been defeated, and the Israelite army set off through the land to let everyone know of their triumph. At every town, the crowds came out singing, dancing, cheering and waving. There were parties all along the route, and a jolly good time was had by all. Well, nearly everyone. King Saul - always happy to receive a bit of praise and adulation - listened to the songs with a big grin on his face...

'Saul has killed a thousand men,
A thousand men, a thousand men,
Saul has killed a thousand men,
Let's hear it for King Saul!'

Lovely. Just the kind of mass adoration Saul liked to hear. But, the grin faded very quickly when the revellers added verse two. It didn't go down well at all...

'David killed ten thousand men, Ten thousand men, Ten thousand...'

Well, you get the idea. The king was smiling, waving to the crowds and he seemed at peace with the world. But, there were all kinds of unpleasant thoughts going through his head, and most of them involved David being offered the chance to seek new opportunities elsewhere - preferably on a different

planet, ideally in a different life. The more he brooded, the more depressed he became. And who did the courtiers send for when the king was depressed? Why, David of course, to play him a nice tune.

So picture the scene - there is one person you hate more than anyone else in the world, and who walks into your throne room with a cheery smile and a harp under his arm? That's right, Kingly Enemy Number One. Well, you would have thrown spears at David if you'd been in the same situation, wouldn't you? David, realising he was being used for target-practice, dodged the spears, and with great presence of mind decided that soothing music was off the menu for the rest of the day.

Saul tried other plans. He sent David out to fight in situations where he was guaranteed to die. Unfortunately, nobody had read the terms of the guarantee to God, and he sent David back safe and sound every time. The people of Israel saw a hero who just couldn't stop winning. Saul saw someone who was now much more popular than he was. The throne wasn't big enough for the both of them. Someone had to go and the king was fairly certain it wasn't going to be him.

Saul's next move seemed to be a bit of a U-turn. It's a big jump from throwing spears to offering to be someone's father-in-law, but that is exactly what Saul did. David was understandably surprised to be offered the promotion from soothing-song-singer to royal prince and brother-in-law to his best friend, and he wasn't sure he was the right sort of person to marry the king's daughter. Saul was the king, though, and he would have his way. The wedding day was set, the invitations issued, and David had just gone for a final fitting for his wedding waistcoat when he heard the news that Saul had married off his daughter to someone else! It was all very puzzling. Had he thought too much about the whole thing, David might have worked out that the king

was playing with him. One minute Saul was all hugs, huge welcomes and 'Let's get related.' The next it was tantrums, tempers and flying spears. A strange business all round.

Besides, David had other things on his mind. He had been very flattered to be offered the chance of marrying Princess Merab. His joy was spoilt only by the fact that he was in love with her younger sister Michal. Michal loved David, but how could they marry? Of such stuff, the plots of soap operas are made.

When Saul learned of the romance that was sweeping through the palace corridors, he began to plot again. Stories from his childhood filled his thoughts, stories of would-be suitors being sent on desperate quests in order to win the hands of their lady loves. Only in Saul's mind, the story would have a different ending. He imagined the hero being brought back to the palace in several sacks, having a decent period of public mourning (five minutes would do the trick) and relaxing in the knowledge that the threat to his throne had been removed. The difficulty was choosing the right task for David. Killing the giant would have been the obvious one, if he hadn't already done that. And there was a severe shortage of dragons in Israel. In the end, the best Saul could come up with was a cunning and - he hoped - deadly plan. It went like this - if David killed one hundred Philistines, he could marry Michal. Surely, out of one hundred Philistines there would be one who could get in a lucky[13] shot?

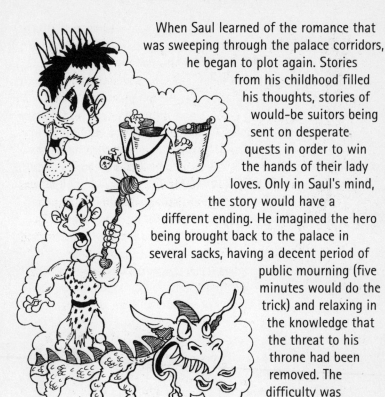

---

[13] Lucky for the Philistine that is... not for David.

FOUR SKINS? NO, I'VE GOT 200 HERE!

Apparently not. It seemed that David had only been gone five minutes when he was coming back with enough evidence to show that he had killed two hundred Philistines. (What exactly it was that he chopped off the dead bodies to provide the proof, we shall leave tactfully on one side. You, I hope, live in a polite and well-bred society where such things are not discussed.)

Saul had to let the marriage go ahead, but it seems fair to say that he was not the happiest father-of-the-bride in the history of royal weddings. His worries about David threatening his position as king grew and grew. His frustration turned to anger, the anger turned to fury and a plan began to form - a plan that would remove David, and leave the path clear for Jonathan to start 'King-training school'.

5 THE PLOT THICKENS

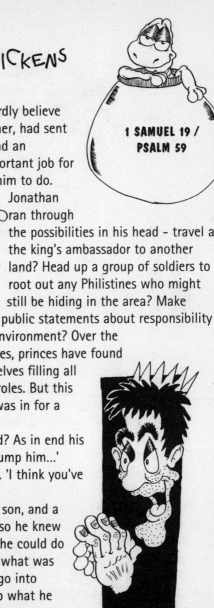

**1 SAMUEL 19 /
PSALM 59**

Prince Jonathan could hardly believe his ears. The king, his father, had sent for him, saying that he had an important job for him to do. Jonathan ran through the possibilities in his head – travel as the king's ambassador to another land? Head up a group of soldiers to root out any Philistines who might still be hiding in the area? Make public statements about responsibility to the environment? Over the centuries, princes have found themselves filling all these roles. But this prince was in for a shock.

'Kill David? Kill? David? As in end his life? Put his lights out? Bump him...'

'YES!' roared the king. 'I think you've got the idea.'

Jonathan was a good son, and a loyal servant of the king, so he knew there was only one thing he could do – he went and told David what was happening, urged him to go into hiding and promised to do what he could to sort the situation out.

The next day, with David safely hidden in a field, Jonathan took his dad for a walk in the very same field, so that David could hear for himself what was going on. Jonathan made a quick summary of all David's achievements, pointing out that he was probably the best supporter the king had. The sun was shining, the birds were singing and all seemed well in the world. For a moment, the king's mood lifted and he agreed with Jonathan that killing David would be a bad move.

Saul and David didn't actually kiss and make up (thank goodness) but it seemed that they were going to be able to get on together. David continued to show that he was a valuable member of Saul's army. But jealousy and anger are strange things to allow into your life. Like computer viruses, they can lie dormant for ages, and then with a change to the calendar or a double-click on the wrong icon, they spring in to life bringing chaos and destruction to everything they touch.

What pushed Saul's button on this particular evening we'll never know. David was halfway through his regular medley of 'songs to calm the troubled breast', when a noise caught his attention. He stopped in mid-verse, and looked up to see the familiar sight of a flying spear... coming straight at him.

David ran from the king's rooms, clutching his harp and any other bits that needed protection. The spear stuck in the wall. Luckily, one thing was certain - it wasn't stuck in David... this time.

That night, Michal heard a noise and looked out of the window. Lots of palace guards were coming down the path. She was sure they hadn't come for tea and biscuits (not at that time of night, anyway). David had told her about the frequent trouble at the palace, but now it looked as if the trouble had followed him home.

She woke David, and helped him sneak out of a window at the back of the house, and then set about trying to distract the soldiers. The old 'dummy in the bed trick' might seem a bit obvious to us in these sophisticated times. In those days, it was new enough to fool them every time. Throughout the night, soldiers who glanced into David's house, saw what they assumed was him sleeping - as long as they knew where he was, they were happy. The king's orders were to kill him at sunrise.

By the time sunrise came, David was a long way from home, and Saul was inspecting the expertly stabbed mattress that the soldiers had brought back. Saul was not a happy man, and he wasn't going to leave it there.

David ran and ran until he saw the prophet Samuel's home. Samuel had started all this in the first place, so, thought a tired, hungry and (if we're honest) a slightly anxious David, it was up to him to do something. When Samuel heard what was going on, he hurried David off to a place known in those days as 'Prophet World', a sort of early theme park for those seeking religious fun and excitement.

Whether it was the gathering of so many godly people in one place, or just one of life's peculiar mysteries, strange things happened to those who crossed the town's boundaries. The soldiers who came searching for David found themselves rolling around on the floor, yelling out a mixture of prayers, religious words and one or two non-religious ones. It was all highly embarrassing - trained soldiers, highly-skilled fighting machines, suddenly turned into a local cabaret for the curious and terminally bored. The whole fabric of the known world seemed to be being torn apart. Prophets were meant to prophesy and soldiers were meant to...er, well soldier and all this confusing of roles was not going down well.

In the end, the king decided he would have to step in, which is exactly what he did, and all he managed to do. One step through the town gates and he found himself rolling on the ground, ripping his clothes and screaming out all kinds of strange words and phrases.

For those who wanted to think about it, there was a message here: God was looking after David, and David knew that only by staying close to God was he ever going to be kept safe. While the crowds gathered around the latest street-entertainer (who turned out to be King Saul) David found a quiet corner and wrote a song...

OH! THAT POOR MAN CANNOT AFFORD ANY CLOTHES!

THEY'RE NOT MAKING THE PROPHETS THEY USED TO!

PSALM 59

Saul is trying hard to kill me
And the thought just doesn't thrill me
Violence - there's a thought to chill me!
Enemies creep up at night.

My future's looking none too bright.
Eternal God - you know my plight.

Let me laugh and sing your song
Only you can keep me strong
Rescue me - I know you're near
Deliver me from all I fear.

6 A FRIEND IN NEED

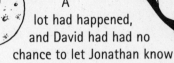

1 SAMUEL 20

A lot had happened, and David had had no chance to let Jonathan know what was going on. The New Moon Festival was coming up, and this would give David the chance to try an experiment that would bring his best friend up to date with all the news.

During all this time, Jonathan had been away from the royal courts. The last time he had seen his father and David, they had been making a new start in a cornfield. As far as he knew, everything had gone well since then. Which is why he couldn't believe what he was hearing when David found him and told him all that had happened. 'My dad tells me everything,' insisted Jonathan, 'I would have known.' But there was something about David's manner that made him wonder whether the dad/son bonding process was really as strong as it should be.

'If your dad has my best interests at heart, then he would expect me to go home to Bethlehem for the festival,' said David. 'So if I'm not at the palace banquet tomorrow, and you tell him that is where I have gone, he should be pleased.' This made sense to Jonathan. He agreed to tell the king that David had returned to Bethlehem. It all seemed perfectly straightforward, but as David pointed out, 'You may hear things you don't want to know. If you find out your dad really does want to kill me... whose side are you going to be on?'

For Jonathan there was no contest. He promised David that nothing would break up their friendship, and outlined his own plans for making sure that David would escape if he really was in danger. These plans were sure to include at least three of the following:

Jonathan would question his father closely.
Jonathan would let David know everything he found out through a secret arrow code.
Jonathan would hope to still be alive at the end of all this.
Er...
That's it!

The next night, Saul eyed the empty place at his banqueting table. Normally he would have been glad to be in any room where David wasn't, but now he wanted David where he could see him. If there were troubles, David seemed to be behind them. True, Saul admitted he'd turned up trumps over the Goliath problem. The trouble was, as far as Saul could see, that David was becoming a bit of a giant himself in the people's eyes. Saul didn't know much about kings, but he knew that in most countries there was only room for one. In his country that meant him.

When David still hadn't turned up on the second day of the festival, Saul began to smell a rat (and it wasn't one that had been served up as a starter).

The king turned to Jonathan and, in as innocent a voice as he could manage, asked, 'Where is that dear son-in-law of mine?' Jonathan gave the story that he and David had agreed on - a family dinner, very sorry not to be there, humble apologies etc.

If Jonathan still entertained any thoughts that David was getting the king completely wrong, they were blown to smithereens by his father's reaction to this news. Jonathan had heard the word 'traitor' and the phrases 'you should be ashamed' and 'wish you had never been born' uttered by his father on many occasions, but they weren't usually directed towards him. He wanted an explanation - and he got one. It arrived by air mail. It looked like a spear. It flew through the air like a spear.

Jonathan was pretty sure it was a spear. He got the point (or rather he didn't - which was just as well). He was convinced that David was telling the truth.

The next day, Jonathan, as arranged, set out for where David was hiding. He couldn't go and speak to David openly in case his servant rushed back and told the king where he was. Instead, he shot his arrows over the fields, sending his servant to find them. As the boy bent down to pick up the arrows, he heard Jonathan shouting, 'They're further on, keep going.' The lad gathered the arrows together thinking, 'What's he going on about? They're right here. A bit too much of Saul's special brew at the banquet - that's his trouble.' Of course, being a good slave he kept his thoughts to himself. After all he didn't want to lose his job - or his head.

David, in his hiding place, heard Jonathan shouting, and immediately understood what was being said. This had been the agreed code to let David know that his life really was in danger. Waiting until the servant had been sent back home with the arrows, David came and had a final word with Jonathan. Their friendship had lasted many years, and the time they had spent together was precious. Now one would have to live the life of an outlaw, and the other would have to live in a palace where, at any moment, the king's violent mood swings could mean disaster for everyone. They stood there together, saying their goodbyes; two young men both appointed to be king - one as a result of his birth, and one by God. Only one of them could be king. Who would you go for?

David soon discovered the joys of life on the run - plenty of fresh air (sleeping in it), fresh water (wading through it) and fresh food (hunting it). He couldn't help thinking that life as a shepherd had been alright, really. Sure there was the occasional prowling lion, but they didn't usually throw spears, and when David was around, they didn't prowl for too long.

He had left his home for what seemed like a top job. Now he wasn't welcome at court, he'd had to leave his best friend, and there wasn't any sign of that crown that Samuel had promised him.

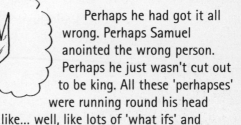

Perhaps he had got it all wrong. Perhaps Samuel anointed the wrong person. Perhaps he just wasn't cut out to be king. All these 'perhapses' were running round his head like... well, like lots of 'what ifs' and 'maybes'. But underneath all these confused thoughts there was a stronger voice, a calmer voice. A voice that assured him that God does not make mistakes, and even if there was a long road to run down, David would be back in the royal court, sitting on the throne at the end of it.

7 UP-CLOSE AND PERSONAL

The life of an outlaw was not easy at the best of times, and David felt ill-equipped for the role. His hasty departure from the palace meant that he and the few men he had gathered to go with him were now homeless, weaponless and - rather more importantly, judging from the noises coming from their assorted stomachs - foodless. The priest in the town of Nob (residents were known locally as Nobbers) was a little surprised to see David and his men enter the town, but soon accepted the story he was told of the men being on a secret mission from Saul (so secret that even Saul didn't know about it).

1 SAMUEL 21:1 – 22:5

RUMBLE!

44

Ahimelech, the priest, looked at the crowd of... well, soldiers he assumed, but they looked a bit dusty and bedraggled to qualify for fighting force of the year. They wanted food and he would have loved to give them food, but as he explained...

'It's like this lads. I've got a few loaves, but they have already been offered to God on the altar, and rules are rules. I can only give them now to people who are pure in mind, body and spirit. I don't want to be too critical but... well, you could all do with a bath...' Before he had a chance to finish, David had jumped in and assured Ahimelech that it would be difficult to find a purer body of men (providing you didn't look too hard). Ahimelech didn't want to argue the point, and so handed the loaves over.

As the men settled down to their makeshift supper, David noticed that one of Saul's shepherds was worshipping at the altar. Doeg was loyal to the king, and tough enough to take on David and his men without a second thought. David's gang had to get away quickly before they were seen. They were just making their way to the town gates when David suddenly realised they didn't have any weapons - did Ahimelech happen to have any to spare? There was a sword as it happened - Goliath's sword, a relic of David's great victory. If it belonged to anybody now, it was surely David's.

He took it and was well on his way before Doeg got to the end of his prayers.

In Gath, David thought that he had found a place of safety. Unfortunately, his reputation had arrived there before him, mainly passed down in those jolly victory songs that had upset King Saul so much. The people of Gath had heard about the tens of thousands that David had killed, and assumed that he must be the king in his own country. In those days, people were a suspicious lot. A king didn't visit the king of another land just to pass the time of day. He usually had other intentions, generally involving killing, killing and anything else that came to mind - probably more killing. David had to act quickly, and did the thing only a wise man would think of - he acted like a fool.

Those who saw him lying by the town gate dribbling (with a skill that would have attracted the attention of the local football team[14]) down his beard and muttering all kinds of nonsense, couldn't quite believe that this was the king who had come to conquer them. They rushed to tell Achish the King of Gath that there was a madman at the gate. 'Tell him I've already got plenty' was the king's reply. Not the funniest joke in the world I know. Quite honestly, though, if you were around the king when he made a

---

[14] Not that there was one... but you knew that, didn't you?

joke, and you wanted to still be alive to hear the next one, you laughed.

While the court of Gath discussed David in terms of his being 'three sheep short of a flock', the 'mad king' had made his escape to a hermit's cave near Adullam. What the hermit thought of this refugee harpist coming to take over his cave we may never know, but it was here that David had a chance to stop, take stock and think about his next move.

Over time, while he sat and thought, others came and found him - other Israelites on the run who were looking for a leader; those who had had enough of King Saul's increasingly bizarre behaviour; and most importantly, David's brothers. Suddenly, from being on the run with a handful of men, David discovered that he had become the leader of over four hundred men. Four hundred men who were well equipped (and willing) to face whatever Saul decided to do next.

Saul's soldiers tried to look as though they were listening as the king ranted on. They had heard it all before. 'Disloyal to the king... blah blah blah... even my son betrays me... drone drone drone... I've been a good king... so on and so forth.' Doeg, who had been at Gath when David had come asking for food, decided he ought to tell Saul what he had seen. For although David had thought that he had escaped unnoticed, Doeg had, in fact, seen him running away from the town. Doeg told Saul all about the help that Ahimelech had given David. For Saul this was the last straw - if even the priests were against him, what chance did he have of getting anywhere?

1 SAMUEL 22:6–23

DO YOU THINK I LOOK FAT IN THIS?

He sent for Ahimelech and repeated his 'How could you do this to me' speech. The priest listened patiently, and then argued David's case. 'David is loyal to you, he's loyal to God, you couldn't hope for a better person to be on your side.' But Saul wasn't listening. He had got to the point where he truly believed that everybody was conspiring against him - priests and all - and he wasn't going to put up with it. 'Kill them,' he roared. It took those who were standing around a while for it to sink in - Saul meant kill the priests... the people of God... the holy ones. Nobody moved. If there was going to be any slaying of priests, nobody wanted to volunteer. Nobody but Doeg, who not only killed all the eighty-five priests who had come with

Ahimelech to see the king, but then travelled to their home town and killed everybody and everything there. An over-reaction? A bit harsh? These were tough times, and for all the blood shed that day, David was still alive. And while he was alive, Saul was not going to be a happy man.

In the game of cat and mouse being played across Israel, David definitely had the advantage - he had God on his side. God had already outlined his plans for David's future, and wasn't about to let him get caught in an ambush or even a bacon tree[15]. So wherever David went, Saul would

1 SAMUEL 24

---

[15] Ham bush – bacon... geddit? Oh never mind.

eventually find him. Or at least he would find the place where he had just been. Every time Saul arrived at David's last known location, David (advised by God) had moved on. If this was a game, it was a game which Saul was determined to see through to the end, despite knowing in his heart of hearts that God's plans would always win through in the end.

David was camped with his growing band of outlaws, family and general hangers-on in Engedi when he heard that Saul was on his way with a huge army. In fact, Saul had three thousand men, and he marched them up to the top of a hill and he marched them down again. (Of course, that could have been someone else - I get confused.) Anyway, they were getting near to David's hideout when Saul suddenly found himself much nearer than he realised...

An army, they say, marches on its stomach (which probably means that most school cooks have been in the army because if you've eaten their cooking, it feels like an army is marching on your stomach). Be that as it may, every fighting force has needs - to eat, to sleep and to pay a visit / use the facilities / spend a penny / go to the

smallest room – however you say it, they all had to do it. Even kings. (The agonies of sitting through a long journey with your legs crossed and desperately trying *not* to think of rushing waterfalls, dripping taps and cool mountain streams is not unknown to even the most royal of royals... What's that? ... All that talk of water has what? ... Oh, alright off you go, I'll wait ... Finished? Good. Did you flush and have you washed... OK! I'm only asking!)

King Saul was no exception. If he had to go, then he had to go, and just at the moment he had to go.[16] So he nipped into the nearest cave and proceeded to

adjust his clothing and deal with the matter in hand. I won't go into too much detail, but I'm sure I don't have to draw you a diagram. Strangely enough, the very cave he had chosen for his royal bog was not in fact unoccupied. In modern times, the discreet word 'engaged' at the entrance would save such an embarrassing moment, but those kind of facilities were a long way from being developed.

---

[16] A man's gotta poo what a man's gotta poo!

At the back of the cave, listening to every groan, every sigh of 'my word, that's better!' and the scuffle for the toilet paper, were David and his merry men. David's companions urged him forward. God had promised him that his enemies would be defeated, and what greater enemy was there than King Saul?

David crept towards the king with his sword in his hand. Any noises he made as he moved were covered by the noises Saul was making (which we don't need to go into). Soon David was right behind the king. He could have ended his life there and then, but he knew that whatever anybody else did, he had to do what was right. So quietly and quickly he cut off a piece of Saul's robe and scurried back to join his gang.

Once Saul was out of the cave, David's men started having a go. 'How could you have done that?' 'Why didn't you kill him while you had the chance?' 'Are you mad? What's that brown lump on your shoe?' The questions came thick and fast, but David knew he had done the right thing. If God wanted to deal with Saul then he could, but David was not going to decide in advance what God did and didn't want him to do.

David left the cave and saw the king marching away into the distance. He shouted and Saul's army stopped. They were so surprised to see David appearing from the very cave where their king had just been, that they didn't move and listened to David's words.

'King Saul, what do I have to do to convince you I am *not* your enemy? I could have killed you in the cave but I didn't.' As he said this, he waved the piece of the king's cloak to show how close he had been. 'Who is doing the *right* thing here? Evil men do evil things as the proverb says. *Who* is doing the evil thing?'

The soldiers were ready to attack David, but Saul stopped them. For a brief moment, he saw the foolish way he had been acting lately. If God really was going to make David king, it would be an act of madness to stand in his way. Saul asked David just one thing: 'Spare my family. Let them live.' With David's words of assurance[17] ringing in his ears, he took his three thousand men all the way home. David went back to his hideout and waited to see what God had in store for him next. While he waited, he did what he had done so many times before at important moments in his life - he wrote a song.

---

[17] An easy promise to make. It had been the habit in those days for new kings to wipe out all the members of the previous king's family, but David wasn't like that.

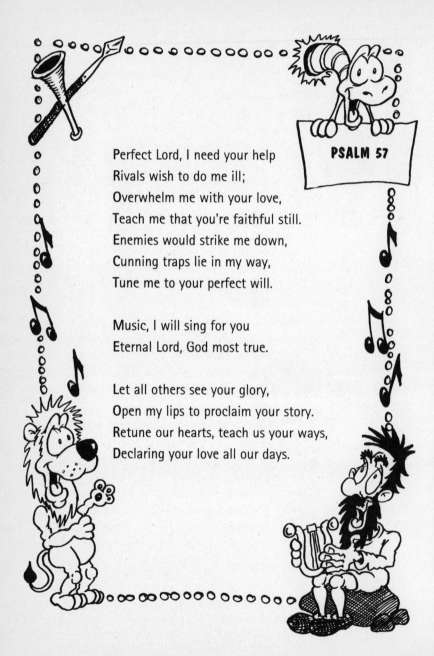

Perfect Lord, I need your help
Rivals wish to do me ill;
Overwhelm me with your love,
Teach me that you're faithful still.
Enemies would strike me down,
Cunning traps lie in my way,
Tune me to your perfect will.

Music, I will sing for you
Eternal Lord, God most true.

Let all others see your glory,
Open my lips to proclaim your story.
Retune our hearts, teach us your ways,
Declaring your love all our days.

PSALM 57

8 A FEAST FIT FOR A KING

1 SAMUEL 25

It was one thing to have reached an agreement in the hills, but David wasn't convinced that the time was right to walk back to Saul's royal court, pick up his harp and continue where he had left off. After all, David had promised to spare Saul's life, but nobody could recall there being a similar promise made by Saul. For the time being it was safer to stay in the hills.

David's life hadn't turned out how he expected it would when Samuel had told him that he would be king all those years ago. Now Samuel had died, but David still held on to the promise of God's good plans for his life. But when you are living in the desert, and constantly on the run, God's promises don't feed empty bellies, and the rumbles from the stomachs of David's men were getting louder and louder.

YODEL-HEY-HO-HO

David, however, had a plan. When he had been an honoured guest in Saul's court (rather than the complete pest Saul had turned him into), David had got to know a lot of people. In this world, it is so often the case that it's not what you know but who you know that counts (although

I've always found that it's what you know about who you know that usually brings results). David had been friendly with a rich landowner called Nabal, and his wife Abigail. In fact, when David wasn't trying to avoid capture by Saul and his armies, he always made sure that Nabal's shepherds were looked after, that his sheep were kept safe and that nobody came to any harm. So you'd think that a simple request for a bit of food, a spare blanket and one or two other provisions would quickly have been okayed, wouldn't you? How wrong you would be!

Nabal was having none of it. He might have been prepared to rub shoulders (a strange Middle Eastern custom) with David when he was in Saul's good books, but there was no way he was going to upset the king by offering hospitality to some runaway low-down, dirty dog. He told David's servants straight: 'How do I know that David has sent you? Who is David, anyway? For all I know you could simply be scroungers on the make. I've got my own family to think of, I can't be doing with you - GET LOST!' If all this has a fairly modern ring to it, you've been listening to the wrong kind of people say the wrong kind of things about asylum-seekers, refugees, the homeless... in fact, anybody who is in need. So stop it now...OK?

One of Nabal's servants heard all this and he was not happy. Never mind the fact that

IS HE SHEARING?

NO! DOESN'T LOOK LIKE HE'LL SHARE ANYTHING!

David had been a good friend to them - there was always the question of what he would do to them now. Why would he go on protecting the shepherds and the flocks if he never got anything in return? Something had to be done, and the servant knew just the person to talk to...

ALL I WANTED WAS A PERM!

Behind every successful man, there is usually a very surprised woman and Nabal's case was no exception. When the servant told Mrs Nabal (her friends called her Abigail, her really close friends called her Abi) what was going on, she didn't think twice, but set about preparing the sort of picnic you always dream of having on a school trip. There were loaves of bread, enough lamb to cause a mint sauce shortage, raisins and figs for those who were on a healthy eating kick, and some good wine to wash it all down (now I come to think about it, maybe it's not quite the thing for a school trip to the zoo after all). The food was loaded on to donkeys and sent to David's camp (with a little note pointing out that the donkeys weren't part of the supper, and should be returned at David's convenience. Although why you should want to keep your donkeys in your toilet is anyone's guess).

The food arrived not a moment too soon. Not because David and his men were about to die from hunger, but because David had just made up his mind that he was going to have to get rid of Nabal and all the other men and boys who lived and worked with him. When David got cross, he went for it in a big way (as Goliath had found out). As David was working out his battle-plan, the first donkey arrived with Abigail on its back. She explained everything. 'It's all been a terrible mistake. Nabal obviously doesn't know what he's doing. I hope that there won't be any hard feelings. Oh, by the way, I understand that God has something special lined up for you, which I am sure will come about. When it does, don't forget who brought you the food, will you?'

I don't know... it seemed that people only did things in the hope of getting something in return. Nabal wouldn't help David because he wanted to keep on the right side of Saul; Abigail *did* help David because she wanted to be on *his* good side. If I were God, I'd wonder why people don't just do what is right because it's right? Not that you or I would be guilty of acting with such mixed motives... Oh dear me, no.

So it was that David ate, Abigail returned home in safety and all was nearly well... but not quite. Abigail eventually plucked up courage to tell Nabal what she had done. The news didn't go down well. It wasn't just Nabal's gasp of surprise; it wasn't just the groan that passed his lips; nor was it the fact that he clutched his chest and fell to the floor that gave the game away. It was more the combination of all three things that made Abigail start thinking 'Wind again!', I mean 'Heart attack!' It wasn't quite the end of Nabal - he lasted another ten days before he closed his eyes for the last time. Plenty of opportunity for him to think about what might have been. If only he'd been a bit more generous when David came knocking. He would just have to hope that God wouldn't be quite so abrupt when he came knock-knock-knocking on heaven's door. I feel a song coming on.

And did David remember Abigail like she had asked? Remember her? *Remember* her? He married her!

Those of you who have been following the fortunes of David closely will remember that he already had a wife back in Saul's palace - Michal - the one who had helped him escape from her father's soldiers all that time ago. So why rush into another marriage? Had all those

MARRIAGE MARKET

days in the hills wiped the memory of his first love from his mind? Or had he just gone along with the mood of the times which seemed to say 'If they take your fancy, marry them and who cares what other people think?' Possibly the latter - I don't want to completely destroy any idea you may have that David is the superhero of the Israelite nation, but Abigail was not his first stroll down the bride aisle of his local marriage-market. I didn't like to bring it up earlier, but David had, in fact, also married someone from Jezreel called Ahinoam.

Just in case you're starting to feel sorry for Michal, I ought to point out that while David had been practising being the Robin Hood of his day, her father had found her a new husband... so I suppose everybody was happy. But it all seems very complicated to me. How on earth they would have sorted out who visited who at Christmas and New Year remains a complete mystery. Mind you, if you think David was a bit of a ladies man, I ought to point out that in years to come, his yet-to-be-born son (Solomon) would leave him standing. *He* ended up with seven hundred wives and three hundred concubines (who were a sort-of 'almost-wives' for whenever he had a spare moment... as if!).

Oh, and if you are wondering about Solomon's mother... she was a wife that David hadn't even met yet! Honestly, sometimes I think these stories should come with a health warning. Having sorted all that out, let's move on... wives and all.

NO! THAT'S A COMBINE!

9 THE KING IS DEAD

1 SAMUEL 27

Life was becoming increasingly difficult for David. Being on the run all the time really took it out of him (not to mention his growing family, and all the demands they made on him) and he needed a safe place to hole up. It was time he paid the Philistines a visit. There were plenty of Philistines who remembered the encounter with Goliath, and felt that if David had a good side, it was best to keep on it (to make sure he wasn't carrying a sling and stones).

No self-respecting Philistine leader who liked the way his head was attached to his shoulders was going to refuse David and his gang a safe place to stay. King Achish was no exception. We're back in the land of people doing things for selfish reasons. It might have been fear that led the king to lay out the Welcome mat, but he soon realised that having David as a pal was better than having him as an enemy.

HMM. I THINK HE'LL SPOT THE BEARTRAP

For the sixteen months that David was living in the area, King Achish's (try saying that out loud... it sounds like a sneeze but that's not really important) view on the whole affair was coloured by the little white lies[18] David told him. (Sorry to have to break it to you, but eventually you'll get the picture that David is not quite the hero you think he is.) He would set out on raids of other local towns, killing the Philistines, and bringing back the food to feed his army. Just an everyday story of outlaw folk. The only difference was that David was telling Achish that he was attacking the people of *Israel*. If Achish had heard stories about the Philistines and the Amalekites being polished off left, right and centre, then it was nothing to do with David. Achish believed that David had had enough of his own people, and was now prepared to wipe them out. It seemed to him that if he played his cards right, then David would become a very useful fellow indeed to have on his side. Sadly for Achish, David still had his eye on the top job in Israel and the date for his coronation was not that far away.

---

[18] OK, whopping great fibs, if you insist.

One day, Achish saw his opportunity to enlist David in the Philistine army attacks on the Israelites. David seemed to go along with the idea. Whether it was all a cunning plan of his, we cannot be sure because, as we shall see, events (as so often in this tale) turned out a little differently than expected. However, for the time being, David had his men line up with the rest of the Philistine troops and off they set towards Saul's army.

From his camp in Gilboa, Saul could see the thousands upon thousands of Philistines just waiting to attack. At the sight of these massed ranks, he felt his innards turning to water, his legs becoming jelly and an

HELP!

overwhelming desire to climb into a dark hole for ever. And in this terrified state, he did what most people do when life seems to be getting a little tricky - he cried out to God and had all his folks do the same. He humbled himself; he prostrated himself before the Holy One; he prayed all the prayers he had ever learned, and one or two that he made up on the spot. Basically he shouted out to God 'Help!' - but no answer came. Not even a reassuring message like,

I'M SORRY, THE CREATOR OF HEAVEN AND EARTH IS BUSY IN ANOTHER PART OF THE COSMOS AT THE MOMENT. PLEASE LEAVE YOUR NAME AND NUMBER AND A MESSAGE, AND HE'LL GET BACK TO YOU AS SOON AS HE CAN. THANK YOU FOR CALLING AND HAVE A NICE LIFE.

Saul felt terribly alone. He had taken God's help for granted for so long that it was a bit of a shock when suddenly it wasn't there. It never occurred to him that perhaps it hadn't been there for a long time. He'd been so busy doing his own thing, his own way in his own time, that God had been left out of the picture for too long. Now it seemed as though God had dropped out of the frame altogether. Who else was there to turn to? Well, Samuel, of course - he seemed to know how to dial the right codes and get through to God every time. Perhaps he would...

But no, Saul remembered, there had been a big funeral, lots of mourners and Samuel had, as it were, been guest of honour. Now Saul came to think about it, Samuel had been the dead centre of attention... literally. But there were those around the land who claimed to be able to talk to the dead. Maybe it wasn't too late to get in touch with Samuel, and just maybe Samuel would make reassuring noises - just like he used to do all those years ago (when he was alive).

Now, anyone with even a random scattering of brain cells might have realised that if you want to get back into God's good books, then what you don't do is to start doing the very things that he has said are a bad thing[19]. For example - mixing with mediums[20] and witches comes high on God's 'don't even think about it' list. As may have been obvious for a while, Saul had not only lost his marbles way back, but he'd mislaid the bag they came in and torn up the rules of the game. It will come as no surprise, then, to learn that when his servants told him about the witch at Endor, that's

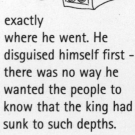

WITCH OF ENDOR. SHE HAS A TWO BROOMSTICK RATING AND THREE TOADS ON OFFER!

exactly where he went. He disguised himself first - there was no way he wanted the people to know that the king had sunk to such depths.

---

[19] And before anybody points out that Saul is already in God's 'Good Book' – the Bible... I know... it's just an expression. Can I get on please?
[20] People who say they can talk to the dead.

It was unfortunate that some time before, Saul had issued instructions to do away with all mediums, fortune-tellers and anybody whose working life involved the use of crystal balls, strange herbs and dark incantations. It meant that those who had survived - including Euphemia of Endor (or whatever she called herself) - were a bit wary of fortune telling and casting the runes for any Tom, Dick or Saul who came calling late at night. Saul persuaded her that it would all be all right, and asked if he could speak with Samuel.

Imagine Euphemia's surprise when Samuel actually appeared - usually it was all done with mirrors, subtle lighting and other tricks of the trade, but now it had all gone out of her control. How he had got there, she had no idea, but it was nothing to do with her.

Saul told the spectre of Samuel what he wanted, and the ghostly prophet replied with words that Saul had heard before but never really listened to. 'You were disobedient, Saul. You went your way, not God's and so God looked for another king and found him in David. It doesn't matter what you do - you will never defeat him. In fact, quite the reverse. Anyway, don't get too down about it. We'll soon be able to have a good long talk about it... only this time at my place, if you get my meaning.' Then he was gone, and Saul never even got to ask for a second opinion. In fact, he didn't get to ask for anything, because Euphemia Ectoplasm found him squirming on

66

the floor in terror. Before daylight, he had recovered a little, but nothing could take away the horror of what he had heard. God had not just left him for a while, but had abandoned him for ever and there was nothing he could do.

1 SAMUEL 29,30

Saul wasn't the only one who was having what passed for a bad hair day in those times.[21] Over in the Philistine camp, just as Achish was feeling good about his secret weapon (David, remember?), things began to go pomegranate-shaped[22].

The soldiers came to Achish and explained their problem. 'You see,' said their spokesperson, 'we're a bit wary of this David. This, after all, is the same David who a while back was slaughtering our armies. We're just a bit... well, put it like this if he were a bear and he suddenly turned up claiming to have turned vegetarian,

WHO'S FOR PUDDING THEN?

---

[21] The Philistines knew all about those. In fact some years before they had given Samson a never-to-be-forgotten haircut. See *'A Tent Peg, a Jawbone and a Sheepskin Rug'*... if you dare.

[22] It would have been pear-shaped, but they only had pomegranates.

would you invite him into your tent for a cheese sandwich? I don't think so. We want him out of here... permanently.'

David heard about all they said and did his best to look astonished and innocent, with a 'Who me? The very idea... as if I would even have thought of such a thing' expression on his face. Achish was completely taken in by this. It's not for me to judge whether this gives us an idea of David's acting ability, or the high stupidity factor of Achish. But let me put it this way - I wouldn't be looking for David's name among any Oscar nomination list.

David and his soldiers had wives and families waiting for them in Ziklag, so this seemed like a good place to go. Or so they thought. At the end of their three day journey, as they were dreaming of tea by the campfire, catching up with their kids' archery practice and spending some quality time with their beloved (or, in David's case, beloveds), what they actually found was a town that was a smouldering ruin and neither sight nor sound of any family activity.

Either somebody had left the gas on when they were last in town, or there had been an enemy attack. Given the shortage of gas meters, broken pipes and naked flames, David decided on the latter option. He knew the work of the Amalekites when he saw it, and he was looking at it right now. His soldiers were not happy.

said one.

added another. Even the smallest soldiers at the back of the crowd could be heard muttering.

Not the kind of comments to inspire confidence, especially when they were threatening to lob bricks at him as well.

David called on his priest to do whatever was necessary to offer prayers to God asking for advice. Like so many people, David turned to God when he was in trouble. We also know from some of the songs he wrote that he also talked to God when things were going well (ah - if we could only say the same thing about ourselves). Anyway, the long and the short of it was that God told David to go for it - to hunt down the Amalekites - and that his family and the families of the other soldiers would be rescued.

The men were tired and weary after their three-day march, but the thought of finding their wives and children gave new strength to most of them and off they went. There were two hundred men who said, 'I couldn't walk another step' and didn't, but that still left David with an army of four hundred men, so he wasn't too alarmed. The most important thing was to discover where the Amalekites were. What they needed was, speaking off the top of my head, a slave from the Amalekite army who could be persuaded to co-operate. Well, blow me down and call me Freddy if that isn't exactly what happened.

The lone Egyptian they found starving in the wilderness turned out to be just such an abandoned slave. He had fallen ill on the journey from Ziklag, and was considered too much of a hindrance to take any further. The Amalekites were in a real hurry to get away, and because this slave was chucking up, they chucked him out.

With a bit of bread, fruit and some water, the slave was ready to take them to his leader. All he asked was one thing. 'Please don't kill me. Don't give me back to my owner,' which pretty much meant the same thing.

When they found the Amalekites, there was a bit of a party going on. The element of surprise, and the amount of wine that had been drunk by the Amalekites, meant that David's army were soon celebrating another victory. The good news was that their wives and children were all safe and well. Suddenly the mood amongst David's men changed. The conversation went slightly differently.

Being human, the soldiers soon found something else to moan about. They didn't see why the two hundred men who hadn't come with them should get any of the booty they had lifted from their raid. David, however, had other ideas. He reminded his men that it was God who had enabled them to win, and that they ought to do what he wanted. He went on to suggest that maybe God wanted them to share what they had with others. In fact, when he became king (not long now... be patient) he made this idea part of Israel's law, so that there would be no arguing about it in the future (well, that was the idea, but you know how people are - they'll argue that left is right if it suits them. Such people are a dead loss when it comes to giving directions).

Just one little thing to mention - while all this was going on, Saul had been killed. Not by David, as he had feared, nor by the Philistines as seemed increasingly likely, but somebody very close to him - himself. It happened this way...
The skirmish with the Philistines had not been going well -

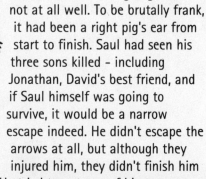

not at all well. To be brutally frank, it had been a right pig's ear from start to finish. Saul had seen his three sons killed - including Jonathan, David's best friend, and if Saul himself was going to survive, it would be a narrow escape indeed. He didn't escape the arrows at all, but although they injured him, they didn't finish him off. He tried to get one of his own soldiers to kill him, rather than be taken by his enemies but the soldier wasn't keen. So Saul got his sword and fell on it... never to rise again. When the soldier saw this, he killed himself too. This was probably an act of loyalty to his king, although who's to say that this soldier wasn't so dim, he

thought he was joining in a royal game? So ended the life of Israel's first king - an event commemorated in the now immortal phrase:

'They think it's Saul over...
it is now!'

10 LONG LIVE THE KING

As Saul gasped his last, there was an Amalekite soldier who had been fighting with his army. I know it sounds complicated, but in those days a lot of soldiers would have joined the side that looked to be winning. Anyway, this soldier was walking over the field of battle at the end of the day, when he came across the bodies of Saul and the other soldier.

The Amalekite soldier realised that with Saul dead, it was time to get into David's good books. So he took Saul's crown, and other identifying bits of clothing, and hurried in search of Israel's 'soon-to-be-king'[23].

When he found David, he told his own version of events, thinking he could perhaps gain even greater favour with him. He told how he had seen the king was in danger, and so in order to save him from capture by the Philistines and all the shame that that would involve, he had killed him. He obviously thought that David would see this as a real act of loyalty and commitment, and that he was bound to reward him - maybe with a minor province in Israel, a few thousand sheep and cattle, perhaps the hand of a beautiful maiden - nothing too over the top, obviously, but enough to let him know that he was appreciated. I don't know at exactly what point he realised his plans had gone wrong. My guess is just before the sword that ended his life came down on the back of his neck.

---

[23] That's David... do try and keep up.

David figured it like this. Even though Saul had done some pretty awful things to him, David had never harmed him, even when he had had the chance. Saul had been God's first-chosen king. He may have turned out to be a bad king, but only God could decide when the time for being king was over. He would have explained this to the Amalekite soldier, but he couldn't... 'cos he was dead. Instead, David turned to his great source of comfort in times of stress and joy - he wrote a song:

'THE SONG OF THE BOW'

Listen all you people,
And heed these words I sing:
Mighty warriors are no more
Evil news I bring
Now Saul's life has been ended
Taken is his son.

Foes will rejoice at our sorrow,
Overwhelming the victory won.
Rush not to speak of our loved ones;

Tell not our news abroad;
Heavy our hearts that even our king
Escaped not the kiss of the sword;

Keep his shield lying where fallen.
Imagine the loss in my heart
Now my friendship with Jonathan has
    ceased
Gone - we who never would part.

It should have been non-stop hop to the royal robe shop for a fitting for David, but - as he knew so well - life was rarely that straightforward. The people of Judah (one of the tribes of Israel) welcomed him with open arms, and the usual bottle of olive oil. Pouring oil over your next king may seem a strange way to behave, but we must make allowances for these quaint practices and customs (after all, I write this in a country where people roll cheddar cheeses down hills, dance with ribbons on village greens and indulge in 'dwile-flonking', whatever that is... actually, I'd rather not know). David was, though, used to all this. Samuel had done the same thing many years before, when he first hinted at a change of career plan for David. All the people of Judah were really saying as they went crazy with the oil was 'Old Sam got it right.'

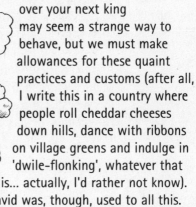

FRY UP!

Mind you, in a twelve-tribe country, being king of one tribe does not automatically make you king of the rest, and there was trouble brewing. Not all of Saul's sons had been killed in the battle with the Philistines. Ishbosheth (if you have false teeth don't even *begin* to try and say this... call him Bob, we'll know what you mean) was still alive. The general of Saul's army, Abner - a man of tradition and ritual - saw no reason why the crown should not be handed over to him as the king's son. He smuggled Bob away from the battleground and had him crowned king of Israel (minus Judah) in a private ceremony, from which all press and photographers were excluded. It wasn't right, and it wasn't what God wanted, but David was prepared to let things run their course. His experience was that God won in the end, and David knew whose side he was on.

There was bound to be trouble. This nation only had room for one king (although God, who had thought the job was his, seemed prepared to let them have one extra) and having two people claiming to be the chosen one only caused unrest, disagreement and some right-royal fallings out. The battles came and went. David had the satisfaction of knowing that he won more battles than Bob, but it wasn't really why he had become king. He wanted to unite the nation, lead them into a new experience of being God's people and try 'living peacefully' as a lifestyle choice for a change.

Still, it wasn't all sword fights at dawn and seeing off the enemy - David, as we have discovered, loved a good wedding - especially if it was his own. Since the last time we discussed his roll-call of wives, he had acquired at least four more. David was clearly a stranger to the concept that you could have too much of a good thing. These wives bore him children, and if he carried on at this rate, he would soon be forming his own thirteenth tribe of Israel.

General Abner was not getting on with King Bob. King Bob had a high regard for Abner as a general. When it came to planning campaigns and rallying the troops, there was no one better. However, King Bob did draw the line when Abner started sleeping with his stepmother, one of Saul's widows. Like many rows, it spiralled out of control, until Abner was stamping his foot and yelling that if that was the way the king felt, then he wouldn't be king for long and he was off to give David the benefit of his advice.

The message got through to David that the general wanted to talk about peace, an idea which was very attractive to David. After all, not only did he want to get on with being king, but he had all his wives to consider, and all the fighting meant that there weren't many nights staying in with the family. He was keen to talk, but there was one condition. Although you would have thought he had enough wives to keep him happy, he hadn't forgotten that Michal - his first wife - had been married off to someone else while he had been running round the country playing hide and seek with Saul.

78

Now he wanted her back. King Bob thought this was a small price to pay to remain king (little did he know) and was happy to make the arrangements. So it was that Michal came back to David - closely followed by her new husband (Paltiel) - who was not a happy man. He sobbed; he wailed; he cried; he poured out his heart - demanding his wife back. The situation needed somebody who would be understanding and caring; somebody who would sympathise with Paltiel without giving in to his demands; the sort of person who wins 'Caring Citizen of the Year' awards. Exactly the sort of person that General Abner wasn't, but it didn't stop him interfering:

PULL YOURSELF TOGETHER MAN, AND GO HOME. WE DON'T WANT YOU ROUND HERE SLOBBERING ALL OVER THE NEIGHBOURHOOD. YOUR WIFE HAS COME BACK TO THE KING AND THAT'S THAT.

Paltiel could take a hint. He got the message and left.

It was a good thing really, as Abner had other tasks to be about, and couldn't afford to waste time on some wimp who couldn't cope with a little thing like his wife being given to someone else. Honestly, they just don't breed them the way they used to. Once Paltiel was out of the way, General Abner was mounting his all-out 'David for king' campaign. He went on a whistle-stop tour of all the tribes, convincing them that David was God's choice for the top job, and that it was time to let Bob go. When he was convinced that the majority of the nation was on David's side he reported back to David and told him to get those coronation robes out - he'd return with the people of Israel right behind him...literally.

There was someone who thought that it was all too good to be true, though. Joab - one of David's right-hand men - was not convinced that Abner was on the level. He thought Abner was probably a spy for King Bob, and someone who definitely shouldn't be trusted. The fact that in a previous battle, Abner had killed Joab's brother, had nothing to do with the matter *at all*. Things were going so well for Abner that when he was summoned to see Joab, he assumed that he had got a message from David for him. He saw nothing wrong with Joab taking him aside - after all, the place was probably crawling with spies and you could never be too careful. He didn't bat an eyelid when Joab got out a knife - you never knew when you could be attacked, and it was better to be safe than sorry. Of course, it was only moments later that Abner never batted an eyelid - or anything else - ever again.

David was not best pleased. He could see why Joab had acted the way he had, but he rather wished that he hadn't. He stormed around the camp wishing all kinds of evil on Joab and his family - boils, pestilence and violent death were just some of the kinder ones. He gave Abner a huge funeral, and appointed Joab chief-mourner (nothing like rubbing salt into the wound) and for the occasion wrote one of his shorter songs...

Died like an outlaw
Except you'd committed
no crime;
Axed like a criminal,
Dead before your time.

King Bob knew that his time was running out. With Abner gone, he became aware of how quickly the tide of public opinion was swinging to David. He thought, though, that he could still trust two of his leaders, Baanah and Rechab. He continued in this happy belief, until they chopped his head off. Like the Amalekite who brought news of Saul's death, these two chappies could see the way the wind was blowing (not a particularly clever trick... most people can do that[24]) and thought they had better get into David's good books.

They obviously knew nothing about the Amalekite soldier, else they might have worked out that David was not too keen on other people sorting his life out for him. He was usually quite content to let God deal with the details, and so far this philosophy had done him proud. Bearing all this in mind, you will not be surprised to learn that when Baanah and Rechab arrived at David's tent with King Bob's head in a bag, he wasn't very pleased. What made it worse was that King Bob had not even been killed in battle. He had been sleeping peacefully, when - WHAM! - no more restless nights... no more nights of any kind.

---

[24] It's easy really: you throw your homework up in the air and see which way it goes. Of course you can't use this as an excuse for not handing in your homework *too* often.

David's response was clear cut - a clear cut through these men's hands and feet, and their bodies were left hanging for all to see. King Bob's head got the full royal burial treatment.

THEY DIDN'T HAVE A LEG TO STAND ON!

And did Bob go to the post-funeral party? No... because he had no body to go with!
Moving quickly on...

11 DANCING KING

It had been more than seven years since Saul's death, but at last the day had arrived. The day Samuel had promised David would come all those years ago. The day when David would be crowned king. And it had been well worth waiting for.

Abner had promised David the people of Israel, and they all turned up. It did mean another lot of olive oil, and the dry-cleaning bills started piling up again, but there could be no doubt about it - the nation had a new king and God showed once again that he could work things out from the most unlikely circumstances and situations. What's more, all the people were on David's side now, and when the cheers went up to greet their new king, the shouts were genuine... from everyone.

Still, there was no time for sitting around thinking how marvellous it all was. There was a job to be done. David had to show his people what sort of leader he was going to be. He looked around for a campaign, a fight, a cause to champion. He found just the thing. The city of Jerusalem had been captured by the Jebusites, and David was just the chap to get it back. God had given his people their land, and other nations had to be shown that they couldn't just walk in and take what they wanted.

So on this coronation day, it was rather appropriate that David was surrounded by a group of well-wishers, because he was, at that moment, wishing they were all down a well... in the nicest possible sense. Let me explain...

Jerusalem was 'well-protected' (be patient, you'll get my meaning soon!), and the Jebusites were convinced that there was no possibility of even David's army getting in there. In a thousand years' time, someone from David's family would ride into Jerusalem, and the people would wave, shout and sing  'Hosanna, the king is here.' For the moment, though, a more subtle plan was needed, which is where the wells came in. The city was 'well-supplied' with water that was piped in through

a series of tunnels. While the Jebusite soldiers were busy peering over the wall looking for intruders, David and his men were right beneath their feet splashing their way to victory.

Before the Jebusites had time to notice that their water had been contaminated with soldiers, it was all over. David had driven the Jebusites out of Jerusalem, and decided that from then on, it would be his city - the city of David. He rebuilt the city according to his design, and set out to rule the people of God. There was also the little matter of the wives. As we have already seen, there was nothing David enjoyed more than adding to his collection of marriage partners, and as he looked around Jerusalem he saw a few more women who he thought would look very nice filling the spare bedrooms of the royal palace. And, as is so often the case (so I'm told), more wives means more children - he had another eleven sons. Of course, this meant finding suitable

WONDER WHY HE'S CALLED ELIPHELET?

names which proved a greater and greater problem. Let's face it any man who names his son - even son number eleven - Eliphelet is rapidly running out of ideas.

Life as king wasn't all extra weddings and being a dad. There was a country to run, a country that was still under attack from the Philistines. David continued to ask God to give him instructions about how best to attack and, surprise, surprise, God always knew best. David didn't just want to kill the odd two or three (hundred) Philistines, though. There was something he wanted to get back... something that had been taken from his people many years before... something that was a sign of how God had chosen Israel to be his own special nation. Something special... and something had to be done...

It had been Moses, the great leader of the people, the person who rescued them from slavery in Egypt, who, having met with God, had given the people of Israel

2 SAMUEL 6 / PSALM 96

God's top ten rules for holy living. Such special instructions needed a special container, and so the Ark of the Covenant had been built. Wherever the people of God went, the Ark came too, as a reminder of how they had been chosen by him. So letting it be stolen had been a bit of a blunder one way or another[25]. The Philistines didn't (for it was they who had stolen it) keep it any longer than they had to. It wasn't that they regretted what they'd done, but that they weren't at all keen on the sores that covered their bodies whenever they got near this holy box. As for the seventy men who died when they looked into it... well, they weren't best pleased either. It had to go back. The Ark had got as far as a town called Kiriath Jearim (try saying that with a mouthful of custard) and then stayed there for another twenty years, while the Israelites got on with fighting, squabbling and arguing about who was going to be king - that sort of thing. Now that it looked as though the arguments were all over, it was time to bring the Ark of the Covenant back home.

---

[25] See *A Tent Peg, a Jawbone and a Sheepskin Rug* for the full story.

There was quite a procession around the ox-cart, onto which the Ark had been loaded. As they got nearer to Jerusalem, so the excitement level increased. David was singing and dancing and it seemed as though nothing could go wrong. Which was why everyone was surprised when Uzzah, son of the man who had been looking after the Ark for twenty years, reached out to steady the Ark when it wobbled, and found himself clutching not the chest of God but his own chest... and dropping down dead. If anybody needed reminding that the Ark of the Covenant was to be treated with special reverence, the evidence was right there in front of them. A very moving sight it would have been too - although, of course, Uzzah wasn't moving at all.

I THOUGHT I'D GET SOME THICK GLOVES... JUST IN CASE.

David began to wonder if he was doing the right thing in bringing the Ark to Jerusalem, and so left it in a little village while he worked out what to do next. Obed Edom became the keeper of the chest, and a very happy man he became too. Once the Ark arrived, it seemed that nothing could go wrong for him: his crops flourished, his livestock bred like rabbits, and his wives started giving birth like there was no tomorrow. So Obed wanted to keep the Ark, but David knew it had to be with him in his city - the city of Jerusalem, which was to be dedicated to the glory of God.

So the journey continued, and the singing and the dancing began again. David got more and more excited - partying like he had never partied before. The more he danced, the more of a sweat he built up. The warmer he got, the more clothing he removed until he was left just in his pants, while everybody looked on and cheered and shouted 'More, more!' (I won't go in to whether they meant more dancing or more stripping.) When I say everyone was shouting, that is to say nearly everyone. David's first wife, Michal, watched it all and she was not best pleased. There was no point in shouting at David now. Who would hear her in these crowds? But just wait until David got home.

'Have you no shame?' she yelled, even before David could walk through the door, 'I've had enough. I've been sold off by my father to another husband; and I've put up with all the other women you've filled the house with. But when I saw you acting like that in the market place, it was possibly the worst day of my life.' But David was not going to be put down. God had made him king and the Ark was back in his city - nothing anybody

89

could say could spoil the day. He didn't think that he would ever forget this day, and just to make sure the memories lingered on, he wrote one of his songs:

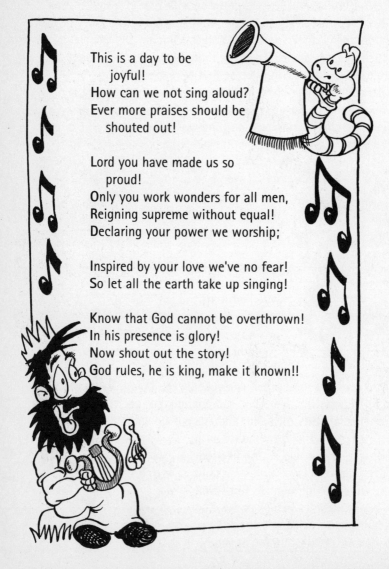

This is a day to be
    joyful!
How can we not sing aloud?
Ever more praises should be
    shouted out!

Lord you have made us so
    proud!
Only you work wonders for all men,
Reigning supreme without equal!
Declaring your power we worship;

Inspired by your love we've no fear!
So let all the earth take up singing!

Know that God cannot be overthrown!
In his presence is glory!
Now shout out the story!
God rules, he is king, make it known!!

David should have been a happy man
- nice palace, good job and
something to hand on to the kids... even Michal
seemed to have stopped sulking about his
dancing. But something didn't
seem right. Here he
was, in his posh
cedar-wood palace
(a designer home for those days... no
TV make-over programme could have
done better) but the Ark of the
Covenant was in a plain old tent.
Surely he ought to do something.
Perhaps
something
tasteful in silver
and gold, with
onyx
trimmings and
marble flooring...
While flicking through a tenth-
century copy of
'Palaces and
Gardens', he was
interrupted by
Nathan, the prophet,
with a message
from God. David
listened as Nathan talked of the God
who had always dwelt with his
people in a tent... who could not be
tied down, but whose sign of his
presence was a home that could be
packed up at a moment's notice to
move on to the next exciting

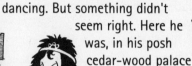

2 SAMUEL 7

ZEBRA PRINT!
LOVELY.

instalment. 'David,' said Nathan, 'I'll be blunt. Don't try and build God a palace - as a builder, you make a great shepherd boy. But don't worry, because God's got a plan, and you'll be remembered alright. Your son will be king, then his son will be king and so on until one day, David, the people of this land will have a king who will be everything you could be to them, and much more. This king will not only be ruler of his people, but of the whole world. In the meantime, it's not the gift of a palace God wants. It's something much more valuable. He wants the gift of your love and obedience... a much harder thing to ask for.'

Asking for a palace, it seemed, was better left to the false 'gods' in the surrounding countries. It was time David and his people thought about giving their whole lives to God's service.

David threw the magazines away and looked at Nathan with an 'I've been a bit foolish, haven't I?' expression across his face. It wasn't for Nathan to tell the king that he was foolish, but he did anyway, making the suggestion that he ought to talk to God about it really, before making a speedy exit. So David did.

The shepherd boy was at last king. He had spent his teenage years looking after his dad's flocks - caring for them, protecting them, leading them to the good grazing places. Now he had a whole nation to look after. Thousands and thousands of people. If he thought about it too much, he became all nervous inside. But then David would remember that this was God's plan, and God's idea, and he would make sure it all worked out.

It was a great thing to know that God was with you, and often, as David lay on his bed at night, he would think about God's other plans - the plans that Nathan had spoken about, the ones that stretched way beyond his own life time. He thought of the king who would come one day. The great King, the true King, God's perfect King. All descended from Jesse's youngest son.

12 BARE NAKED LADY

2 SAMUEL 8 & 9

It was life as normal for David and his army, phlattening a phew Philistines here, and mowing down the Moabites there. He zonked the king of Zobah, annihilated the Arameans and toppled King Toi. In fact there wasn't a king (or a letter of the alphabet) that was safe - from bashing them, conquering them and dancing all over them to walloping them, x-terminating them and yalloping them (OK, I made that one up). David was top ruler and nobody was going to be allowed to forget it.

'PHLATTENING A PHEW PHILISTINES ...'

'... MOWING DOWN THE MOABITES ...'

'HE ZONKED THE KING OF ZOBAH ...'

'... ANNIHILATED THE ARAMEANS ...'

'... TOPPLED KING TOI'.

Sometimes, though, in the gap between skirmishes, David would think about life before he was king. Then he would think about Saul and Jonathan, and wonder about Saul's family and whether any of his family was still alive. Well, there was no point in having a palace full of officials if you couldn't get them to do some work for you. So David sent his spies out for news of his adopted family. The slaves searched high and low. There were plenty of people who claimed to be part of Saul's family. Well, you would, wouldn't you, if you thought it meant a free room in the palace for life? Eventually, one messenger returned and this time it looked like he had found a genuine family member. One of Jonathan's children was still alive. In those days, if you'd conquered a king, then all his family would have considered themselves as good as dead. Most new kings didn't want potential enemies hanging around, waiting for their chance to take revenge. That's why any king wanting to improve his career prospects would make sure that his enemies were hanging around... from the nearest tree. The officials assumed that this was exactly what David would do with Mephibosheth[26] (Jonathan's son), now that he had been found. But David could be a surprising person when he chose to...

A quaking Mephibosheth knelt before the king. It wasn't easy to do, as he was lame in one leg, but he still managed it. As he knelt, he wondered if he was really hearing right. The king was offering him land, servants, and a regular place at the royal table. It was Mephibosheth's leg that

---

[26] We're back in the land of strange names, lots of spitting and the risk of your teeth flying across the room. Treat this name with care.

was lame, not his brain, and he soon realised that the king was totally serious. As we have seen, family - well, in David's case, families - meant a lot to the king and, despite all the unpleasantness, Saul and

Jonathan had been part of his family once. If David had stuck to making families happy, and not dabbled in breaking families up, a lot of unpleasantness could have been avoided. Come on, we're going roof walking - bring your dark glasses - there are some things you might not want to see too clearly...

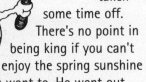

The Israelite armies were off looking for the (very few) places that remained unconquered, and David had taken some time off. There's no point in being king if you can't enjoy the spring sunshine when you want to. He went out

2 SAMUEL 11

onto the roof - you could see a lot from up there. Mothers and children working around the palace, the lands he owned stretching away to the horizon and there below was... good grief! David looked away

quickly. Whoever it was that was having a bath down there probably didn't want anyone looking on. But then again he was king, and who would know if he had a peep? On the other hand, he ought to set the standards for other people to follow. But there was no one else around. And so it was that the shepherd boy turned giant-killer turned outlaw turned king took a new diversion on his career path... a right royal creepy peeper[27].

The woman was called Bathsheba (if it had been raining when David spotted her, perhaps she would have been called 'Showersheba'... but then again maybe not). Her husband was away fighting for the king. David had enough wives to keep him busy, and he should have just left Bathsheba to get on with her life. But you know how it is - you think of what you would like to do, tell yourself you mustn't, think that nobody would get hurt, then keep on coming back to the original thought. But part of you keeps saying 'Go on... you know you want to.' You're probably thinking, 'Don't even think about it' but which part of you will win? It will come as no

---

[27] Centuries later a chap called Tom peeped out as Lady Godiva did her famous horse-back streak through the streets of Coventry. He was struck blind for his cheek. But David was a king and he was not going to be struck blind. Oh no, the consequences of this particular peeping day were going to be much, much worse.

surprise, then, that before the day was over, Bathsheba found herself in the king's bed. And she wasn't alone.

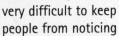

That should have been that. Another royal scandal, hushed up because the servants wanted to keep their jobs. Unfortunately, events took a sudden turn, and the deceit could not be kept quiet. It wasn't that Bathsheba talked about what had happened, and David certainly wasn't bragging about his, er, little lapse. However, once you are going to have a baby (and oh yes, Bathsheba was) it is very difficult to keep people from noticing that you are getting larger and rounder. What's more, if your husband is away fighting a war, then this baby is unlikely to be the result of him sending you an extremely passionate love letter. Tongues would begin to wag, the gossip would start and the people's minds would have but a single thought: who is the dad?[28]

David had to do something. His plan was to call Uriah (Bathsheba's husband) back from the army in the hope that he would spend the night at home with his wife making up for lost time (if you get my meaning). Then it would be easy to point to the baby and make loud comments around Uriah like 'Ooh, he's got your eyes.'

David had reckoned without Uriah's sense of loyalty. He was on active service for the king, and as far as he was concerned, active did not mean the kind of activity the king was suggesting.

---

[28] I know we know but this book wasn't around in David's time.

While he was on duty, there wasn't going to be any 'hanky' let alone 'panky' until the battle was over.

SORRY SIR! COULDN'T DO THAT SIR!

David was not going to be beaten - perhaps getting Uriah drunk would work.

Typical really. You spend your life encouraging your soldiers to be loyal and focussed, and then when they've got the

NUTTER!

SHORRY SHIR! SHTIL COULDN'T DO IT SHIR! HIC!

hang of it, you can't get them to unlearn their basic training. Uriah, despite being drunk, still refused, and slept on a blanket in the palace guardroom. But time was passing, and the baby's presence would soon be obvious. Desperate measures were called for, and David took them. He ordered Uriah to be put in the front line of the next battle. If you wanted someone to be bumped off, this was going to be as good a place as any - and

HE'S DEAD? BOO HOO!

TOP SECRET ORDERS.

so it proved. When David heard the news, he put on his 'Ah well, you win some, you lose some' expression, although deep down inside, there was a part of him that was all fists in the air and yelling: 'YESSSS!'

Bathsheba acted just as a grieving widow should. But when the mourning was over - early afternoon, I presume - David added her to his list of wives, and his son was born. If there were those around the palace who could think back nine months from the birth, then they were keeping very quiet. It had been a risk, but it looked as though David had got away with it.

MOURNING'S ALMOST OVER!

Well, actually he hadn't. The 'nobody will ever know' line can never work if God is watching what is going on (and he always is). So it wasn't too long before Nathan turned up with another message from God for the king. He told the king a story, that went something like this:

2 SAMUEL 12:1–23

Gonna tell you a story 'bout a man named Fred,
Could earn a million shekels without getting out of bed.
He was rich, he was loaded, he was rolling in the stuff,
But no matter what he earned he could never get enough
(gold, that is).

OF GOLD THAT IS

FRED Nearby his neighbour was trying to get by,
He'd nothing in the bank - 'twas enough to make you cry,
His problems were enormous and would make anybody fret,
The only happy times he had were playing with

NEIGHBOUR his pet
(lamb, that is).

The lamb was treated kindly
by the poor man's family,
They were kind and they were loving, what
a family ought to be,
They often missed their meals but they
didn't seem to care,

LOTS OF LOVE For the one thing that
mattered, they had plenty
of to share
(love, that is).

NO TEA

Well the rich man had some
friends round who were stopping for their
tea,
The rich man knew they looked to him for
hospitality,
He thought for food he'd raid his flocks, then had a
better plan,
He knew someone who had a lamb
and he'd steal it from that man,
(the poor man, that is).

NASTY THOUGHT The rich man's friends enjoyed their
meal, especially the main course,
The little lamb tasted so sweet
when served up with mint sauce,
While next door the poor man's
family were searching high and
low,
Where their little lamb had got
to, they really didn't know
MINT SAUCE (but we do).

THE LAMB, THAT IS!

LOVE, THAT IS

THE POOR MAN, THAT IS

BUT WE DO!

Nathan was about to launch into the final chorus, when David shut him up with a right royal roar: 'That's outrageous!' he stormed. 'Absolutely diabolical! Preying on the weak and treating them so badly. If this wasn't a story, I'd have the rich man brought here and I'd... I'd... chop his thieving hands off'.

Nathan, who - as we have seen - was never one for holding back when things needed saying, looked at the king and said quietly but firmly:

'It is no story, and there is such a man... you are the man.'

David's gast had never been so flabbered! When had he ever taken a lamb that wasn't his, when he didn't need it? People's flocks and livestock were safe while he was king!

'Maybe so,' said Nathan, who thought he had better see the whole thing through, 'but people's wives are not so safe are they? God knows how you took advantage of Uriah's wife, and then arranged to have him killed. You had so much, and yet you still wanted more. Compared to you, the man in the story was only dabbling in the waters of despicable behaviour. You are in it right up to your neck.'

David could hardly speak as Nathan went on outlining the consequences of his sin - division within his family, the loss of his wives - and here was the most important point: David had tried to hide what he had done. What God was planning to do would be seen by the whole kingdom, and while he would allow David to live he would allow his newborn son to die.

It is indeed a terrible thing to act in ways that displeased God, as David was beginning to realise. He cried out to God; he went without food; he prayed through the night, begging that his son might be allowed to live. It seemed as though heaven - once always alert to David's cries – had shut its doors and refused to listen. When the child died, David had a choice – he could have sat around feeling sorry for himself, or he could have got on with trying to make the future a better place than the past. But first he needed to let God know how he was really feeling. He had written plenty of songs of praise, of faith and hope. Now he wrote a song that showed his heart to all who listened:

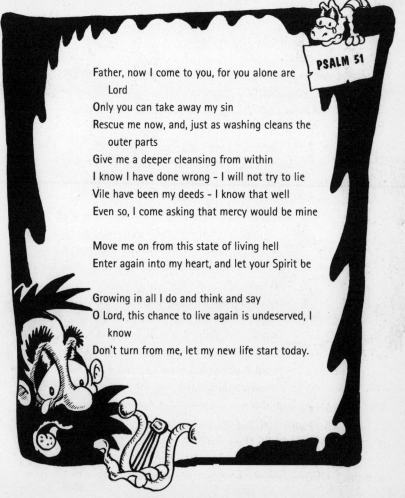

PSALM 51

Father, now I come to you, for you alone are Lord
Only you can take away my sin
Rescue me now, and, just as washing cleans the outer parts
Give me a deeper cleansing from within
I know I have done wrong – I will not try to lie
Vile have been my deeds – I know that well
Even so, I come asking that mercy would be mine

Move me on from this state of living hell
Enter again into my heart, and let your Spirit be

Growing in all I do and think and say
O Lord, this chance to live again is undeserved, I know
Don't turn from me, let my new life start today.

13 FAMILY STRIFE

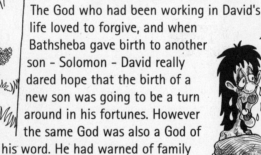

The God who had been working in David's life loved to forgive, and when Bathsheba gave birth to another son - Solomon - David really dared hope that the birth of a new son was going to be a turn around in his fortunes. However the same God was also a God of his word. He had warned of family strife, and family strife there was going to be. David had collected so many wives (to be honest, I've given up counting) that it was almost inevitable that there would be lots of children (and there were). Remembering who belonged to who, and how everyone was related, was a time-consuming business, and not everybody could be bothered - David's son Amnon for one. He had fallen in love with his half-sister Tamar, which was definitely against the rules (then and now). But he clearly inherited his father's belief that if you want something, then nothing should get in the way of you having it... not even Tamar's screams and struggles as he tried to overpower

104

her. She knew this was wrong, and she knew she should try to stop what was about to happen, but though she fought Amnon was definitely the stronger and she couldn't prevent it.

When it was all over, she went to see her real brother, Absalom, in shame and disgust. He wasn't happy about what had happened, but thought it better to keep quiet, or the whole family would be caught up in the scandal. Absalom acted as though nothing had happened. Any onlooker would have thought how marvellous it was that step-children could get on so well. But inside, Absalom was smouldering with anger. And the problem with smouldering anger is that, given time and the right circumstances, it erupts into the full blown flames of hatred.

It was sheep-shearing time when the fire began to lick round Absalom's heart. Amnon was working with Absalom and all their brothers - enjoying the work, sharing the wine and even beginning to believe that his stupid behaviour with Tamar was all in the past. When Absalom's servant started waving a knife around, Amnon didn't think he was about to offer to cut the crusts off the lunchtime sandwiches. Amnon's past started to flash before his eyes. He realised that there wasn't going to be a future. It is possible that the last thing

Amnon thought before death carried him off was, 'What's that knife doing in my stomach?' We may never know.

Absalom did not regret what he had done, but he knew that his father, the king, would not approve. The rest of his brothers left the sheep-shearing and rode for their lives - after all who knew where Absalom would tell his servants to start sticking knives next? But for now they were safe. Absalom rode off in the other direction.

For three years, Absalom lived with his grandfather (you could look back and find out which of David's many wives was the daughter of King Talmai, or you could just take my word for it). It seemed that David was never going to forgive him.

NO GRANDAD YOU HAVEN'T TOLD ME ABOUT THE GOOD OLD DAYS

At the same time, David was listening to an old woman telling him how her sons kept falling out, and how difficult it was to get them back together again. He only half-listened to her tale of a divided family, and spent most of the time thinking about his own. As the woman droned on, it suddenly occurred to David that he was being set up. Joab, the commander of his army, had been on at him for months to sort things out with Absalom, and this was clearly his latest attempt. The old woman didn't deny it - she had indeed been drafted in from Rent-a-crone, and Joab was standing nearby to see how the king would take it.

RENTA CRONE

Very well, as it turned out - he told Joab that

Absalom could return to Israel. However, just to make sure that Joab still knew who was king around the place, he refused to see his son.

For two years, David and Absalom lived in the same city without bumping into one another. In the end, Absalom decided to make the first move and wanted to use Joab as a go-between. Joab, though, knew exactly how the king felt about seeing Absalom. He wasn't going to risk his job - let alone his life - by getting more involved than he already was. Until Absalom set fire to Joab's crops that was.

It is a fairly desperate way of getting the attention of someone you want to speak with, but it works every time, and this was no exception. So Joab persuaded the king to meet his son. After five years of division and bitterness, David and Absalom got together again. There was hugging, kissing and all that kind of stuff. It seemed the rift was healed. But as later events were to show, appearances can be deceptive.

David may not have seen much of Absalom, but Absalom made sure everybody else did, and those that did got a very good impression indeed.

2 SAMUEL 15:1 – 16:14 / PSALM 3

107

Slowly, over the months and years, people started to think more of Absalom than they did of their king... which was just the way Absalom wanted it.

People riding to the palace for advice from David would be stopped by this good looking, long-haired prince, who would take their sides in disputes, and always ensure that they got the impression that

their cause was right and just. Had there been a poll for most popular Israelite, then Absalom would have been the runaway winner. Instead, he simply decided to run away.

Of course, he didn't let the king know that he was doing that. Oh dear me, no. David thought Absalom was going to keep the promise he had made to God. Absalom, though, was in Hebron and the people were flocking to his side. If there was going to be a takeover, then they wanted to be on the winning side, and at the moment it looked as though Absalom would come out on top.

When David heard that Absalom was marching on the city with his army, he didn't wait around to see if they were coming simply to pay respect. He took the men who had remained loyal

with him and, pausing only to pick up the Ark of the Covenant, he left Jerusalem, wondering how much worse the situation could get. It was a bit late for 'if only's' but he couldn't help wondering how different it would all have been if, on that fateful day on the roof, he'd kept his eyes and hands to himself.

Bringing the Ark with them was slowing them down, and David had it sent back. He knew that God alone could work things out, and if he was allowed to return as king, then all well and good. But if not... then the people would still need God's law - they could always find a new king.

Not everyone had joined Absalom. Here's just a few of those who hung around for one reason or another:

ITTAI - not an Israelite, but on David's side.

THAT'S 'GITTITE' AND NOTHING SHORTER THANK YOU!

"ITTAI THE GITTITE"

HUSHAI - prepared to spy for David in Absalom's camp.

THAT'S HUSSSSSSHAI THE SPY, SO KEEP IT QUIET

ZIBA - (MEPHIBOSHETH'S SERVANT) - made sure King David was kept supplied with food and donkeys (what more could a man want?).

Mind you, Ziba brought bad news along with the food and the donkeys -

HOPE THEY KNOW THE DIFFERENCE BETWEEN FOOD AND DONKEY

Mephibosheth had stayed in Jerusalem. Not to fight off Absalom's armies, though. Oh no, he foolishly believed that when Absalom arrived, he would hand over the kingdom to Mephibosheth, as Saul's surviving grandson. It was all very confusing - there was plot, counter-plot and a lot of double-dealing going on.

David travelled on, looking for answers, and trying to find a way of solving this crisis. He needed to be sure that God was still prepared to use him. When he was stoned by Shimei[29] and his people he couldn't help feeling that he deserved it. He had not been the faithful ruler of Israel he had intended to be, and if God was determined to punish him, then he was not going to fight back.

David was still able to put his feelings into song, but they had more of an abrupt quality, probably because he was on the run:

How many are my
enemies?
Endless is my strife
Lord be my shield,
both day and night,
and please
Protect my life

---

[29] Ed. – not our highly esteemed narrator, Shimei the Smelli.

14 HAIR-RAISING EXPERIENCE

2 SAMUEL 16:15 – 19:14

Things were really hotting up, and the race for the crown was on. Hushai arrived in Jerusalem about the same time as Absalom, and persuaded him that he was on his side now - because God was on Absalom's side now. For a holy man, Hushai was a jolly good liar. Mind you, a few miles away David was beginning to wonder whether God *was* on Absalom's side. Had his disastrous involvement with Bathsheba ruined things forever?

Hushai was doing all he could to make sure that Absalom's plans would come to nothing. He set himself up as a sort-of battle-plan advisor, and did such a convincing job that this pretender to the crown was completely taken in. Whatever, it seems, that David had done in the past, God had not finished with him yet.

Hushai was a busy fellow. No sooner had he finished persuading Absalom that David would be in one place, than he was dashing off to get the message to David that he needed to be in another. Ahithophel, who until now had been Absalom's chief advisor, did not take kindly to being replaced as top strategist. Most of us suffering such a disappointment would have gone off in a sulk, locked ourselves in our bedroom and played loud music or just kicked the nearest

111

cat. Not Ahithophel - when he sulked, he did it big time. People thought he was quite upset. When they found him hanging outside his house one morning, looking very blue around the lips, they knew they'd been right.

Still, no time to worry about dead chaps - there are living ones to keep an eye on, and a kingdom to be won. Absalom was preparing for the final push. He moved his men into position, and began to make speeches about fighting on beaches, fields of human conflict and the last one back is a big cissy. At the same time, David had arranged his troops into three groups under the leadership of Joab, Abishai and Ittai. The question about which group he should join was decided by the army commanders, who decided that since the whole point of this exercise was to make sure that he ended up king again, it would be better if he stayed alive and not join any of them. So David waited while his men marched off to the final conflict (until the next one).

It was in Ephraim Forest that the two armies met, and as the fighting

> **I'M READY TO FIGHT THEM ON THE BEACHES NOW!**

went on, it became obvious that David's men were winning: this only meant that less of David's men were killed than Absalom's. It wasn't much comfort at all to those who were breathing their last to know their side was winning.

As the day wore on, Absalom discovered he really should have paid a visit to the hairdresser's before he started to fight. The people of Israel admired his long flowing locks, but they weren't a lot of use when riding through forests. Suddenly, in the middle of the battle, Absalom had a strange uplifting feeling and watched as the mule he was riding rode off through the forest, leaving him dangling by his hair from the branches of a tree. It didn't take him long to 'twig' (sorry - I just can't help myself sometimes) what was going on, but there wasn't much he could do, except hang around and wait to be rescued... or killed. Killed seemed the likeliest option, as David's men were the first to pass by. But that is exactly what they did - pass by. War or no war, nobody wanted to be the one who had to own up to killing the king's son. Nobody apart from Joab, who didn't think twice about thrusting a spear through Absalom's body... in fact he thought about it three times: once for each spear. Then he sent in ten more men to finish him off. A bit over the top, but that's life... or rather death.

With Absalom's death, the fight was as good as won. The big question now was, who was going to tell the king? Zadok's son, Ahimaaz, favoured the tactful, 'break it to him gently' approach, which would have gone well if some passing Ethiopian hadn't come rushing up, yelling:

HE'S DEAD, DEAD, DEAD! AND YOU CAN BE KING, KING, KING!

David could have begun his triumphant march back to Jerusalem. He could have ordered a great celebratory banquet for all who had stayed loyal and fought for him. He could have declared a national holiday. But instead he sat down and cried. He cried for his dead son, but also for all the thousands of others who had died, and for his own mistakes and failures which had meant that God's purposes had taken a bit of a pounding.

Joab was not impressed. What the people wanted was joy and celebration. They wanted to be

114

told how well they had done, not to think that their fighting had reduced their king to tears. He got hold of David, and told him to get out where he could be seen and for heaven's sake - SMILE!

When the news of the victory spread, the people of Judah were instructed to make the arrangements for David to return to Jerusalem. It was time for the king to come home.

15 GIVE PEACE A CHANCE

2 SAMUEL 19:15–43

The journey home was full of meetings.

There was Shimei who, the last time David had passed his way, had spent the time throwing stones at him. Now the stones were in the other hand, so to speak, and David had a pretty good reputation where stones were concerned.

Shimei begged to be spared, although David's commanders urged him to end Shimei's life. But David was in a good mood

- he was the king of the castle, and just for the moment there was no dirty rascal in sight. So David told Shimei he could go, and continued his journey to Jerusalem.

THIS TIME HE'S BOUND TO KILL ME!

The next person he came across was Mephibosheth. The last David had heard, he had been siding with Absalom. Mephibosheth denied all knowledge of this, and declared himself glad to see the king again (wouldn't you?). David had already promised the lands he had given to Mephibosheth to Ziba (his servant) but now decided they could split them fifty-fifty. Keen to

116

underline his loyalty, Mephibosheth said Ziba could have them all – he was just glad to see the king was still alive. I suspect Mephibosheth was glad that he was still alive too, and that may have had more to do with his generosity.

It wasn't going to be a quiet life. The history of the world tells us that no matter how often blood is shed, there will always be those who still fight, argue and squabble, laying the foundations for the next great battle. So it was that David's grand arrival home was marred by the people of Israel and the people of Judah debating over who should have brought the king back. Somehow, David knew the days ahead were not going to be peaceful.

And so it proved – Sheba, from the tribe of Benjamin, shouted louder than the rest of the Israelites, and persuaded the people to follow him. David could spot the seeds of rebellion at fifty paces, and so one of the first things he did when he got home was to send his soldiers off to do a spot of bud-nipping. He asked Amasa to 'amassa de troops' (tee-hee) but he seemed to spend a long time getting it sorted. In the end, Joab and Abishai went to sort out the problem with Sheba. There was a sneaking suspicion that Amasa was taking a long time because he wanted to let

2 SAMUEL 20

Sheba get away. Joab knew how to deal with problems like that. He used a knife, and the problem was last seen lying in a pool of blood. 'A mass a' blood you could say... but we won't.

Joab found Sheba in the town of Abel, and surrounded the place. The inhabitants were a little scared, to say the least. All except one old woman, who suddenly appeared at the top of the town walls, shouting for Joab's attention. 'Young man,' (she certainly knew how to flatter), 'just what do you think you are doing?' Joab may have had a short fuse when it came to spies, rebels, enemies and other unpleasant people, but he always had time for old ladies. He explained who they were looking for, and assured her that her town, her family and that little something she kept under the mattress were all perfectly safe. Once she realised Joab only wanted the rebel they were hiding, she cheered up considerably. 'If you want Sheba, then Sheba you shall have.' Sure enough, she was as good as her word, and only a short while later the head of Sheba came flying over the walls. Admittedly, there had originally been more to him than that, but Joab was fairly certain that he wasn't going to be causing any more trouble.

Joab blew his trumpet and off they set for Jerusalem. And the rest... well just your usual kingly stuff really - dealing with famine situations, appeasing nations that had been wronged by a previous king, giving Saul a decent burial, planning the building of a temple (which Solomon[30] would have the task of seeing through) and fighting off assassination attempts. All in a day's work. But most of the time there was peace - forty years of peace, and that left plenty of time for writing songs.

FAMINE, APPEASING NATIONS, BURYING KINGS, PLANNING TEMPLES! WHAT WILL WE DO TOMORROW?

---

[30] Number 2 son to Bathsheba and David.

LAST BITES

Before we let the sun set on David's reign, we'll hear one more song. But before that, let me just tell you that although David had learned and relearned to trust God (and...), he was still prone to forget sometimes that if he had achieved anything, it was because of God's protection and direction. When all was going well and the nation was at peace, it was a bit too easy to sit back and think 'Man, I've got it made.' It was something like this that led to him sending his men out to count the nation. Not so that he could praise God for all who had come under the Lord's rule and reign, but so that he might feel good about having so much.

David was impressed with the numbers. God was not. David had blown it again. But one thing he had learned was that God was always willing to listen if you wanted to start again. All those years

528,366... 528,367... 528,368... **WILL YOU KEEP STILL?!! WHERE WAS I... NO! I'VE LOST COUNT!!**

ago, God had looked on the inside not the outside. He had looked at David's heart. He saw in David then, and went on seeing, a young man who for all his mistakes, pride, foolishness and sin, longed to see God at work in his life. A man who knew that without God he was nothing. A king who was learning to think God's way, even if going God's way wasn't always easy. It was these attitudes that interested God. He could work with someone like that. If someone was prepared to come to God and say 'Sorry, let's start again,' then God knew that something could be done. He's the same God who wants people to start again today.

We have even greater reason to believe that God can change us than David did. We know who the great king, ancestor of David, was... You do know don't you? Oh, come on. How many times have you sung the words 'Once in Royal David's City'? Oodles, probably. His city was the town of his birth - Bethlehem. And who was born in Bethlehem? (I'll give you a clue... his name was Jesus!)

WHILE SHEPHERDS WASHED THEIR SOCKS BY NIGHT

Jesus, descendant of David, a king born in a stable, spent much of his adult life wandering the land with no home. He ended his life nailed to a cross. Doesn't sound much of a king? But this was God's King, doing things God's way - which is always a bit surprising. Because that wasn't the end of the story - he didn't remain dead and buried but rose from the dead three days later.

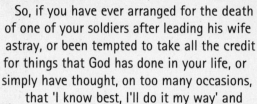

So, if you have ever arranged for the death of one of your soldiers after leading his wife astray, or been tempted to take all the credit for things that God has done in your life, or simply have thought, on too many occasions, that 'I know best, I'll do it my way' and wondered why it all came crashing down - take a hint from David, learn to say sorry and start again.

Remember, Jesus, the greatest King, said 'Come to me, all of you and I will give you rest.' So what's stopping you?

To you, O God, I will sing praises;
Hear my words, receive my song.
All through danger you have protected me,
Never failing me my whole life long,
King of all, your people praise you.

You are faithful, always true,
Only your kindness lasts for ever,
Under your care we have come through.

Listen, now the tears have vanished
Only joy has come from you.
Receive our thanks and songs as we now
Dance before you, Lord most true.

WHO ARE THESE GUYS?

MALC'

Schools-worker, charity coordinator, youth pastor, local radio celebrity, church minister are just some of the 'work experience' that Malc' can fill in on a CV. He has also, at different times, had an ear pierced and dyed his hair green. He devours books, films and black coffee in between working for a church in Coventry, studying in Oxford and socialising with anyone who will talk to him. He has written for SU's *Quest* Bible notes and *SALT* material and now, of course, the blockbuster *Bible Bites* series.

IAN

Shropshire lad, Ian, was born and brought up on a small sheep farm. His childhood dislike of the outdoors, lack of computer games, the everlasting rain and his phobia of chickens (linked to a vicious attack by 300 manic hens when he was four) led him to the drawing board and he's been drawing ever since. Despite his early acquaintances being mainly of the four-legged variety, Ian has progressed through a variety of academic institutions and is now a trainee solicitor working in Sheffield, where he worships at St Thomas's Church.

A Red Sea, a Burning Bush and a Plague of Frogs

In the second book published in the *Bible Bites* series, meet Moses who walked through the sea without getting his feet wet, and who made Pharaoh into a frog-millionaire. I liked it so much I bought fifty copies... but then I ate them all. Belch.

Available from your local Christian bookshop. Or direct from:
S U (Mail Order), PO Box 5148, Milton Keynes MLO, MK2 2YX
Tel: 01908 856006 Fax: 01908 856 020 www.scriptureunion.org.uk

A Ladder, a BBQ and a Pillar of Salt